THE CONCEPT OF RUSSIA
Patterns for Political Development in the Russian Federation

CHAIR INTERBREW - BAILLET LATOUR "EUROPEAN UNION - RUSSIA"

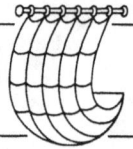

Created in early 2000, the main objective of the Chair Interbrew – Baillet Latour is to encourage multidisciplinary research into the relationship between the European Union and Russia. The Chair Interbrew - Baillet Latour is based on cooperation between the *Instituut voor Internationaal en Europees Beleid* of the Katholieke Universiteit Leuven and the *l'Institut d'Études Européennes* of the Université Catholique de Louvain. Research will primarily focus upon an analysis of the origins, determinants and possible evolutions of Euro-Russian relations. Research is conducted in different fields of study in order to appeal to a large public. The seminars, publications and conferences organised by the Chair Interbrew - Baillet Latour will offer the academic world as well as political actors and policymakers an opportunity to share their knowledge of Euro-Russian relations, primarily from the standpoint of International Relations and History.

As well as organising these activities on a regular basis, the Chair conducts continuous research at each Institute; this will lead to the establishment of a specialist centre at the university and to the promotion of research on the focus areas espoused by the Chair. With this in mind, a Chair Interbrew - Baillet Latour Prize has been established at each university te reward the best graduate thesis on Euro-Russian relations.

Emphasizing the cooperation between the two universities, the Chair essentially works in French and Dutch; where appropriate and depending on the circumstances, English and Russian will also be used.

http://www.soc.kuleuven.ac.be/pol/iieb/ibl/home.htm

Katlijn Malfliet and Francisca Scharpé (eds.)

THE CONCEPT OF RUSSIA
Patterns for Political Development
in the Russian Federation

Leuven University Press
2003

4

Published with the support of the "K.U.Leuven Commissie voor Publicaties".

ISBN 90 5867 345 6
D / 2003 / 1869 / 72
NUR: 754

Illustration cover: Shapka Monomakh. Crown of Monomakh of the Second Order (13th-14th century). Moscow Kremlin Museums.

TABLE OF CONTENTS

PREFACE

In the Spring of 2003 the Chair Interbrew-Baillet Latour at K.U. Leuven organised a lecture series under the title: "The Concept of Russia: Patterns for Political Development in the Russian Federation". Throughout this series of lectures, the Chair aimed to study the never ending search for Russian identity, approaching this multi-layered and diffuse problem from a historical, political, cultural and economic perspective.

Today's Russia profiles itself as an independent, sovereign state, liberated from the yoke of communism and from the burden of international socialist brotherhood within the Soviet state construction. Claiming its membership in the international world of civilised nations, it takes distance both from the old Russian empire and from the Union of Soviet Socialist Republics (USSR). As a New Independent State, it is looking for a clear delineation of its borders, its values, and its domestic and foreign policy. After some hesitation in the early stages of the postcommunist transition, Russia decided that it cannot do otherwise than organise its state in a "Russian way". But how is this typical "Russianness" to be defined? The question, so often formulated by academicians, business people and politicians - "How can we understand today's Russia?" - is indeed rather difficult to answer.

The title of this book is perhaps rather misleading: its phrasing suggests that there is only one way to rightly understand Russia, that there is only one truth about Russia. This is obviously not the case: there is no single and uniquely true concept of Russia. The Russian reality and its development can be approached in many different ways.

The "concept" of Russia refers to the "Russian idea", not as some kind of abstract ideological essence, but rather as principles that are discernible in both thought and social action. It was precisely the partial correspondence between the ideological formulations of the "Russian idea" and the social practices from which these formulations were abstracted that gave credibility to the larger idea of a separate and superior Russian path to modernity. In his book "The Agony of the Russian Idea", Tim McDaniel ponders whether the "Russian idea" can survive within the framework of the current political and economic reforms in Russia.[1]

In their turn, the authors of this book endeavour to follow that same path by going in search of a better understanding of the viability and the widespread loyalty to the "Russian idea".

Geoffrey Hosking and Wim Coudenys approach the "Russian idea" from a historical perspective. Even in its early history, Russia acquired certain features that distinguished it from the West European developments and traditions.

---

[1] McDaniel, Tim, *The Agony of the Russian Idea*, Princeton University Press, Princeton, 1996, 201p.

The impact of the Mongol domination and the early development of the Russian empire, even before its statehood was established, explain several peculiarities of Russian statehood today.

Russia is a state of many peoples: its multi-ethnic definition creates particular problems and opportunities in the field of state building. Professor Irina Busygina describes the incisive and sometimes unexpected reforms recently introduced in the Russian federal structure and organisation.

Staying in the field of domestic politics, John Löwenhardt tries to define certain essential features of Russian post-Soviet political culture. In order to understand contemporary Russian politics, one must examine certain perhaps less obvious aspects that deeply influence Russian society, as for example the harsh climate and the enormous geographical dimensions of the country, the concept of loyalty within the political elite and the militarisation of the leadership.

Dr. Irina Kobrinskaya brings an insider approach to Russia's role in the international security system. She points out the significant role Russia can play in the formation of a new international and European security system, both in the positive sense as an initiator of pacifying measures and as a reliable partner, and in the negative sense as a hampering factor. The development of sustainable relations with the West, and primarily with Western Europe, is a symptom of an increasing pragmatism in Russia's foreign and security policy.

Finally, professor Philip Hanson discusses current developments in economic relations between Russia and the West. After a brief overview of Russian economic developments since the famous 1998 crisis, he provides us with an insight into the present exchanges between Russia and the West in the field of trade, foreign investment and economic freedoms. The perspectives for the Russian economy are rather positive in his view and Russia is clearly endeavouring to strengthen its relations with the West. WTO accession and the creation of a Common European Economic Space may provide the framework within which Russia can take its rightful place on the international scene.

Prof. Dr. Katlijn Malfliet
Research Director Central and Eastern Europe
Francisca Scharpé, Research Assistant

Institute for International and European Policy
K.U.Leuven

LIST OF ABBREVIATIONS

ABM	Anti-Ballistic Missile Treaty
AF	Armed Forces
CEE	Central and Eastern Europe
CEECs	Central and East European countries
CEES	Common European Economic Space
CIS	Commonwealth of Independent States
CMEA	Council for Mutual Economic Assistance
Comecon	Council for Mutual Economic Assistance
Comintern	Communist International Organisation
CPSU	Communist Party of the Soviet Union
EEA	European Economic Area
EMU	European Monetary Union
EU	European Union
Eurostat	Statistical Office of the European Commission
GDP	Gross Domestic Product
GKOs	Russian Government Bonds
GNP	Gross National Product
GSP	EU General System of Preference
IMF	International Monetary Fund
NATO	North Atlantic Treaty Organisation
NIS	New Independent States
NKDV	People's Commissariat of Internal Affairs (Communist Secret Police from 1917 until 1946)
OECD	Organisation for Economic Cooperation and Development
OSCE	Organisation for Security and Cooperation in Europe
PJC	NATO-Russia Permanent Joint Council
RECEP	Russian European Centre for Economic Policy
RF	Russian Federation
RSFSR	Russian Socialist Federative Soviet Republic
SMEs	Small and Medium-Sized Enterprises
UCPTE	Union for the Coordination of Production and Transmission of Electricity
UN	United Nations
US	United States
USSR	Union of Soviet Socialist Republics
UTD	*Uproshchennye Tranzitnye Dokumenty* (Simplified Transit Documents)
WMD	Weapons of Mass Destruction
WTO	World Trade Organisation

INTRODUCTION:
SOME IDEAS ON THE "RUSSIAN IDEA"

Katlijn Malfliet

The aim of this contribution is to provide the reader with some considerations on the various connotations of the concept "Russian idea" which in various forms have been held by the Russian elite down through the centuries. How can we understand this rather odd concept? What are the basic lines of thought that come together in this single concept? How did it originate and develop in Russian society? Can we explain the remarkable viability of this enigmatic concept?

More than a decade after the collapse of the Soviet Union, the search for Russian identity, as a process of self-understanding, is still ongoing. How can we best define Russia's long-term national interests in the fields of political sovereignty, sustainable economic development and military security? How will Russia view its federal state structure, as it finds itself confronted with a centuries-old tension between national and regional identity? Does Russia have to make the choice between East and West? All these questions relate to the centuries-old debate on the "Russian Idea".

One thing has already been sorted out: Russia will not simply copy the Western model of democracy and liberal capitalism; neither will it go back to its communist past. Hence, the question is how the Russian state is expected to develop in the future, what its path of development will consist of, and how specific and original it will be. In order to answer this question - and this answer will always be partial and unsatisfactory - we make an attempt in this book to update the difficult and ambiguous notion of the "Russian idea".

Efforts to delineate a separate Russian path to the modern world go back centuries. For over a hundred years the term "Russian idea" has been in use by Russian writers, academicians and politicians in their search for the basic principles and values that underlie the Russian way of life and deeply influence its institutions and politics. This book will not elaborate on the cultural aspects of the "Russian idea". The interested reader will find a well written evocation of this aspect of the "Russian idea" in Orlando Figes' *"Natasha's Dance"*.[1]

Interestingly enough, "Russianness" is not completely "Russian", as it includes a partial similarity with the "other", while at the same time providing reasons for distinction from that same "other". Even the "Russian idea" itself is not entirely or exclusively Russian (as it contains important principles, such as the responsibility of the government for social welfare, which are west

---

[1] Figes, Orlando, *Natasha's Dance. A Cultural History of Russia*, Allen Lane, The Penguin Press, 2002, 729p.

European in their origin), nor can the idea that Russia itself is distinct from all other nations due to its people's adherence to shared beliefs, community and equality be absolutely true. Nevertheless "Russianness" has always been defined in opposition to something else.

This notion of incompleteness is most probably the result of Russia's physical and psychological location between Byzantine, Muslim and Western civilisations.[2] In Russia, this led to deep insecurity and, hence, to a need to cling to empire, not so much because of its alleged benefits, but because of fear of the unknown.

The "Russian idea" primarily implies self-definition through polar opposition: the West, Russia's "other", is materialist, present-oriented, legalistic and rationalistic. The "Russian idea" can be considered a counterreaction to Western rationality: belief versus incentive, ideology versus dialogue, enthusiasm versus rational planning. Truth (*pravda*) is more important than rules. The law is not perceived as necessarily embodying authentic justice. Therefore laws do not spontaneously need to be obeyed. If government and institutions no longer follow the truth, then they become shadow institutions, deprived of any legitimacy, awaiting their replacement by the true embodiments of the ideal of *pravda*. Hence the authority of institutions and social structures is not so binding in Russia. They are, after all, only phantoms of their true essences. The concept of the Rule of Law, although officially accepted as a basic pillar for political legitimation in the Putin era, is distrusted as being too much the embodiment of the idea of legalism and not always standing for the truth behind this legalism.

After 1830 an enduring controversy about the legacy of Tsar Peter the Great and about the ultimate purpose of the Russian state dominated the debate over Russian identity. The disagreement concerning the image of Peter I in Russian history reflected not so much a dispute about the emperor himself, but rather a basic dispute about the essence of the Russian state.[3] The Slavophiles declared the entire set of Petrine reforms a perversion and a disaster and clamoured to return to true Russian principles, while the Westernisers saw Peter the Great as the victorious creator of the Russian empire, the sage organiser of the state, and the lawgiver of modern Russia.

Russia was long separated from the Western mainstream of German idealistic tradition and enlightenment, mainly as a result of the Mongol Yoke. Westernisers did not believe in a unique political or cultural heritage for Russia: Russia had to return to the European orbit. Russian *zapadniki* (Westernisers) felt quite some ambivalence about reforming the Russian state. While accepting the West as a model and teacher of organisation, they were reluctant to jettison

---

[2] Rieber, Alfred J., "Persistent Factors in Russian Foreign Policy" in: Ragsdale, Hugh (ed.), *Imperial Russian Foreign Policy*, Cambridge, Cambridge University Press, 1993, p. 344.

[3] Riasanovsky, Nicholas V., *The Image of Peter the Great in Russian History and Thought*, New York and Oxford, Oxford University Press, 1985, p. 304.

Russia's political heritage and continued to believe in the viability of the Russian political system, following its own path of development. Most Westernisers never went far enough in their liberalism to question the notion of empire, while the Slavophiles continued to justify the notion of empire through orthodoxy. The Slavophile idea was based on reinforcing the relationship between orthodoxy, autocracy and pan-Slavism. However, in terms of foreign policy, the Slavophiles and Westernisers were both profoundly committed to an ever-expanding Russian empire.

The Concept of the State

In the field of Russian state building, we are confronted with contradictory self-interpretations. On the one hand, Russians can identify the values associated with *gosudarstvennost'* (statehood) as vital to the people's national life; on the other hand, they can portray themselves, as the writer Maxim Gorky did, as an anarchic people, to whom government had to be brought in from outside by the Vikings, the Tatars or the Baltic Germans, for example. The ongoing debate over the origins of the Russian state contributes to Russia's difficulties in delineating a post-imperial nation. Today's Russian students are confronted with this debate in their courses on Russian history and humanities. The cover of a recent handbook, recommended for high schools by the Russian Ministry of Education, on the relations between Russia and the West[5] indeed shows a picture of the Vikings in a fragment of the painting by N.K. Rerich: "Maritime visitors" (1902).

Russia started the building of its empire in 1552-56, when Ivan IV ("the Terrible") captured the Tatar cities of Kazan' and Astrakhan, incorporating for the first time large numbers of people who were neither Orthodox nor Russian-speaking. The early imperial expansion resulted in a continuous blurring of Russian statehood with the idea of a Russian empire, as Russia acquired an imperial identity before it developed a national individuality. The formation of the Russian nation "did not precede the process of Tsarist colonial expansion, but rather coincided with it, the simultaneity of the process blurred the ethnic and cultural definition of Russian nationality, and made Russia's political identity dependent on the Tsarist state's imperial exploits. During most of the twentieth century Russian identity continued to hinge on the international power of the state".[4]

The claim to the legacy of *Rus'* (the ancient core from which the Russian state developed) became so important for Russian identity that most important Russian historians (Nikolay Karamzin, Sergey Solovyev, Vasiliy Klyutchevskiy and George Vernadskiy) have taken the position that Vladimir-Suzdal, and later Muscovy were the true dynastic and cultural successors of

[4] Dawisha, Karen and Bruce Parrott, *Russia and the New States of Eurasia: The Politics of Upheaval*, New York, Cambridge University Press, 1994, p. 26.
[5] Utkin, Anatoliy I., *Rossiya i Zapad: istoriya tsivilizatsii*. Gardariki, Moskva, 2000.

Kievan *Rus'*. This is why the possession of Ukraine, the heart of the lands of *Rus'*, became a vital ingredient in legitimising the Russian identity. A separate Ukrainian national identity was in this way excluded: it was claimed that the inhabitants of present-day Ukraine were Russians.

The "Russian idea" avoids issues of nationalism and national identity and searches for denationalising ideologies. Russia's relentless expansion made colonisation the prime force in Russian history, permanently blurring the distinction between Russia proper and its periphery. All imperial institutions, from the emperor down, referred to themselves as *Rossiyskie*. The term *Rossiyskiy* enabled the Russian intelligentsia to decolourise itself, using the term *Rossiyskiy* (of the lands of *Rus'*) rather than *Russkiy* (ethnic Russian). Russian national identity started to emerge as early as the eighteenth century under Peter I and Catharina II, but contemporary conditions hindered rather than promoted the development of a Russian national identity distinct from the West.

However, Nicolas I's Minister of Education, Sergey Uvarov, was convinced that Russia needed its own national idea, which he tried to build on the notions of autocracy (*samoderzhavie*), orthodoxy (*pravoslavie*) and national outlook (*narodnost'*). Alexander III (1881-94) introduced the notion of "state nationalism" (*kazenniy natsionalizm*), but his embracing of nationalism turned out to be the last gasp of a decadent government. Nationalism became a manipulated state ideology, a product of a small alien minority, while the masses remained indifferent. The word "nationalism" did not appear in print in Russia until the early twentieth century: according to Ilya Prizel, "the regime's preference for an imperial-religious identity, rather than a distinct national one, stems from two legacies: the traditional notion of divine rule, common to imperial European courts, and the non-Russian ethnicity of the Russian court and of the Romanov family. Stressing ethnicity as a source of legitimacy would have merely undermined the *ancien régime* further".[6] A most consolating factor was found in the conviction that Russia, however backward, remained a *velikaya derzhava* (a great power), further linking the notion of Russianness with the imperial Russian state.

Community Life and Christianity

The rulers of Kievan *Rus'* adopted Orthodox Christianity from the Byzantine empire. Russian Orthodoxy instilled a sense of otherness in the Russians vis-à-vis the rest of European civilisation. At the Council of Florence in 1439 the Russian Orthodox Church was severed from its ties with Western Christianity and Moscovy was proclaimed the "Third Rome", a theory and a myth that was later utilised as a justification for imperial expansion. The idea was put forward that the true Christian empire had returned to the East after the fall of Byzantium when the tsar of Muscovy emerged as the strongest of the

---

[6] Prizel, Ilya, *National Identity and Foreign Policy. Nationalism and Leadership in Poland, Russia and Ukraine*, Cambridge University Press, Cambridge, 1998, p.164.

monarchs. As the last bastion of Christianity with a unique mission, Russia had to sacrifice its distinct national identity to a universalist mission associated with imperialism.

When, in the mid-seventeenth century, the priest Arsenius Sukhanov revived the idea of the Third Rome, his motivation stemmed from the discovery of corrupting influences from Latinising and Ottoman pressures.[7] The imperial and messianistic vocation of the Russian Orthodox church remained strong: the mutually reinforcing relationship between autocracy and Orthodoxy was powerful: the Orthodox idea, not the Russian tongue or civilisation, was the *spiritus movens* of Tsardom. Russia was first of all "Holy Russia", not "Russian". The Old Believers despite terrible persecution resisted the Westernisation of the Russian Church and remained true to the traditional church. They became the symbol of integrity, dignity and authenticity.

The "Russian idea" equally contains an assumption of a superior aptitude of the Russian people for community life. Abstract, formal relations based on contract or interest are held to be inferior to warm and deep informal relations based on a strong sense of shared participation in the *rod*, an eternal kinship-community, which unites people to ancestors, future generations and to the larger society, suggesting a fundamental continuity among the life of the individual, the extended family and the larger society.

The sense of community based on membership in the *rod* was held to have religious roots. Russian Orthodoxy, contrary to Western Christianity is characterised by *sobornost'*, a symphonic unity among individual, family and society, in which all elements mutually contribute to the development of the whole. Community, as opposed to law, formal organisation and mutual interest; a fundamentally different concept of the person (*lichnost'*) as opposed to the individual, defines the thinking on social behaviour and social rules.

This sense of the harmonious relationship of the individual to society goes back to the pre-revolutionary *mir*. The *mir* or peasant commune survived the abolishment of serfdom in Russia (1861). This community model was based on the harmonious relationship of the individual to society. In the peasant commune land was not individually owned but rather it was periodically (re)distributed on the basis of family need and size. This essentially egalitarian feature was held by ideology to be typical for the communal nature of Russian society and superior in its principles to Western individualism. War of all against all, which is characteristic of Western society, was avoided in the peasant commune (*mir* also means "peace").

After the liberation of the serfs in 1861, the tsarist government not only preserved, but even extended the rights of the commune over its members. This social practice was able to continue because it was based in a deep

[7] Billington, H., *The Icon and the Ax: An Interpretive History of Russian Culture*, New York, Vintage Books, 1970.

conviction held by the masses: the land belonged to God, and so to the community as a whole, and hence could not be appropriated by private landowners. Among the Russian peasantry, all social relations were defined strictly in terms of a "we versus they" opposition. The communal structure of Russian peasantry made villages de facto extended families, which tended to view all outsiders of a different *rod* and the government (Viking, Tatar, Baltic German or Westernised Russians) as a manifestation of the Antichrist, which allowed little possibility for the emergence of a national identity.

The lingering sense of inferiority vis-à-vis the West drove Russian intellectuals to seek solace in Russia's unique version of Christianity. According to Slavophiles, the absence of a clear national identity leaves the Russian people without national egotism and thus makes them particularly fit to carry out a universalist Christian mission.

The focus in the "Russian idea" is therefore on equality of outcomes: a belief that material conditions in society should not vary too greatly among individuals and classes. Russian emphasis on equality does not mean equality of opportunity because this liberal interpretation of equal rights implies, in Russian eyes, that very unequal results can be perfectly consistent with equality of opportunity. A (Western) liberal view of equal opportunity violates the emphasis on final results as opposed to procedural formalism and it elevates the interests of the individual over those of the group.

Russia's Relation to Europe

Connected with this interpretation of community and Christianity are repeated attempts to follow a different path from Western Europe, to create a society, economy and government that are felt to be more in tune with Russia's own character. The Western path can and should be avoided in the name of a harmonious and egalitarian Russian society based on a higher form of belief. Binary opposition to anything Western is typical for the "Russian idea". Equality versus private property; equality versus individualism, equality versus formal democracy: from its early days, the "Russian idea" was a kind of antibody to modernity, incubated in (Western) Europe (borrowed for example from European social thought), but grown much more potent in its Russian environment.

The problem of the formation of Russian identity is thus closely linked to the question whether Russia belongs to Europe or whether it exists as a separate Slavic or Eurasian civilisation. Most early Russian nationalist intellectuals were educated in Germany and impressed by Hegel's Lectures on the Philosophy of History, in which Hegel divided history into three periods: the oriental, symbolised by despotism; the classical, symbolised by law and order, and the last phase, "man and freedom", dominated by the Germans. The notion of German hegemony was countered by the Russian nationalists with that of a

Russian-centred Slavophilism.[8] Nikolay Danilevskiy, a nationalist strongly influenced by Hegel and an adamant Slavophile, asserted that the third period would be dominated by Orthodox Slavs (not Russians *per se*), who were not as contaminated by western ideas as the "Romano-German" world was.[9] According to Anatole Mazour, "Russian nationalism came as an answer to the fiasco of the cosmopolitan idea of the French revolution and the failure of Napoleon to bring Europe to a federation of states and bend Russia to that scheme."[10] One of the paradoxes and tragedies of Russia's national development was that while the empire was unable to satisfy the growing needs of Russian nationalism, the Russian national consciousness remained fused to the empire.

The Topicality of the Russian Idea

President Putin incorporates the whole binarity of the "Russian idea". Nobody can suspect him of being against market capitalism, foreign investments and the supremacy of the law. His past as a lawyer and security officer, first in East Germany and afterwards in St. Petersburg, where he was responsible for attracting foreign investments, provide him with the necessary credentials. On the other hand, he clearly respected the *nomenklatura* (to which he gave amnesty) and he soon became involved in a titan's fight against the oligarchs surrounding his throne. The hilarious stories with the oligarchs (the Yukos affair beats everything) make clear that economic reforms in Russia are not evolving in the direction of a western market system. Neither can we talk about the Rule of Law in the western sense of the word. Now that large economic sectors are in the hands of oligarchs, who were once authorised to take over from the state, one can again refer to the concept of the "patrimonial state". The judicial fight against politically ambitious "first men" in the economic sector has less to do with western market capitalism than with the myth of the good tsar and the bad boyars. The "dictatorship of law" advocated by Putin, cannot be situated in the tradition of Western legality, but has everything to do with the lack of firm belief in law and the temptation to reduce it to an instrument of power.

Electoral democracy and party pluralism have been introduced, as a mimicry of the West, but how credible is this democracy when a party of the future president, created two months before the election date, wins the elections? This electoral phenomenon does not represent Russia's first steps on the path towards western democracy. Rather it must be explained in terms of the lack of democratic experience with the people and the elite, and the strong autocratic tendencies in Russian society. The same holds true for the media, which have been subjugated to the president, and for the change in the federal organisation aimed at the re-establishment of law and order. In the field of foreign policy, Putin's pragmatism is leading to a multi-vector orientation towards the various

---

[8] Prizel. Ilya, *o.c.,* p. 169.

[9] Danilevskiy, N.YA.. *Rossiya I Evropa,* izd. Glagol', Sankt Peterburg. 1995, XIII.

[10] Mazour, Anatole G.. *Russia Past and Present,* New York. D. Van Nostrand, 1955, p. 30.

actors and regions in the geopolitical field, but Western Europe remains the main strategic partner representing both an example of civilisation and a different path to (post)modernity.

It is probably too early for a judgement on the Putin period, but there are good reasons to forecast that Putin's Russia will remain permeated by the "Russian idea". Power that is based on Russian tradition does not allow for the possibility of placing Russia fully within the context of Western civilisation.

Selected Bibliography

Berdiaev, Nikolai, *The Russian Idea*. New York, Lindisfarne Press, 1992.

Conquest, Robert (ed.), *The Last Empire: Nationality and the Soviet Future*. Stanford, Hoover Press, 1987.

Dawisha, Karen and Bruce Parrott, *The End of Empire? The Transformation of the USSR in Comparative Perspective*. M.E. Sharpe, Armonk, New York, 1997.

Dugin, A.G., *Osnovy Evraziystva*. Moskva, Aktorea Tsentr, 2002.

Klyuchevskiy, Vassiliy O., *Kurs Russkoy Istorii*. vol. II, Moscow, Mysl', 1988.

Lieven, Dominic, *Russia's Rulers Under the Old Regime*. New Haven, Yale University Press, 1990.

McDaniel, Tim, *The Agony of the Russian Idea*. Princeton University Press, Princeton, New Jersey, 1996.

McFaul, Michael, *Russia's Unfinished Revolution. Political Change from Gorbachev to Putin*. Cornell University Press, Ithaca and London, 2001.

Pipes, Richard, *Russia under the Old Regime*. New York, Collier, 1974.

Pipes, Richard, *The Russian Revolution*. New York, Knopf, 1990.

Prizel, Ilya, *National Identity and Foreign Policy. Nationalism and Leadership in Poland, Russia and Ukraine*. Cambridge University Press, Cambridge, 1998.

Rey, Marie-Pierre, 'La Russie et l'Europe occidentale: le dilemme russe', IEE Document no. 32, Louvain-la-Neuve, Juin 2003.

Starr, S. Frederick, *The Legacy of History in Russia and the New States of Eurasia*. Armonk, New York, M.E. Sharpe, 1994.

Tikhomirov, Vladimir (ed.), *Russia after Yeltsin*. Ashgate, Aldershot, 2001.

Utkin, Anatoliy I., *Rossiya i Zapad: istoriya tsivilizatsii.* Gardariki, Moskva, 2000.

Utkin, Anatoliy I., *Vyzov Zapada i otvet Rossii.* Algoritm, Moskva, 2002.

Walicki, Andrzej, *The Slavophile Controversy.* Oxford, Oxford University Press, 1975.

THE STATE AND IDENTITY FORMATION IN RUSSIA: A HISTORICAL ACCOUNT

Geoffrey Hosking

At the time when the Golden Horde collapsed in the late fifteenth century, there were three ways in which *Rus'* might have defined itself: (1) as the successor to Byzantium, guarantor of the Orthodox Christian ecumene; (2) as a nation-state of the East Slav peoples; and (3) as the successor to the Golden Horde, that is, as a multi-ethnic north Eurasian empire. The path actually chosen, mainly for geo-political reasons, was the third. With the collapse of the Golden Horde, northern Eurasia was a power vacuum waiting to be filled, and Muscovy filled it. From the late fifteenth century, then, the Grand Prince of Moscow began to redefine *Rus'* as a north Eurasian multi-ethnic empire. To sustain that role, though, it also had to become a European great power, since in the West it faced the relatively developed states of Europe, without a natural frontier to rely on for defence. In the south and east, the difficulty of securing frontiers in the face of persistent raids by nomadic tribes was even greater. At the other end of Eurasia, the Chinese protected themselves by building the Great Wall. Russians, though, could not do anything similar: any Russian Great Wall would have had to be two to three times as long. So, instead, Russian monarchs constructed fortified lines – *zaseki* – manned by frontier troops.

The consequences of the decision to become an empire were far-reaching. The frontiers were very extensive and, inevitably, embraced many peoples who were neither Russian nor Orthodox. Even as it was taking shape, then, the Russian state became more and more removed from the heartland of *Rus'* and from the Orthodox religion, which had been a very powerful marker of national identity hitherto. During the 16th century the Orthodox people of Muscovy had learned to see themselves as a people chosen by God to save the true Christian faith and to spread it throughout the world. The idea of "Moscow, the Third Rome" was popular in the church and among ordinary people. But this form of national identity was inconvenient to a state which ruled over increasing numbers of non-Christians. During the 17th century the state split the church in trying to modernise it, then subordinated it to the secular power and expropriated most of its property. Divided, subjected and poverty-stricken, the church could no longer function as a guarantor of national culture, even though most Russians, if asked their nationality, would have replied, "We are Orthodox". So, we have the strange spectacle of a population whose national identity was weakened by the growth of empire and by the accompanying process of modernisation from the 17th century onwards.[1]

Research for this paper was made possible by the award of a Leverhulme Personal Research Chair, for which I am very grateful.
[1] Hosking, Geoffrey, *Russia: People and Empire*. London, HarperCollins, 1997, part 2, chapter 1.

At this stage, we have to examine the term "state". Then, it did not mean what we now normally understand by the term. The Russian term translates as "lordship", and that is how Russians saw it, as a mixture of power and ownership. Richard Pipes asserts that this mixture constitutes the defining feature of Russian "patrimonial monarchy", which he considered a uniquely oppressive form of autocracy, in which the monarch's subjects are also his slaves.[2] But this is because he misunderstands the nature of property in 16th century and later Russia. He equates it with the Roman *dominium* and more or less with modern Anglo-American freehold. Actually, the owner of a Russian *votchina*, or patrimony, was restricted in the use of his property by a whole train of traditional obligations, as well as by God's law. Institutions and laws were weak and the Russian state had to conduct its huge task of mobilisation by the use of personal ties and traditional obligations rather than through the unmediated power of the state.

Hence, autocracy actually took the form of hierarchical patron-client relationships. The Tsars provided the symbolic backing of absolute monarchy for the personal power of boyars and, later, nobles to raise armies, levy taxes and apprehend criminals. This method also had the advantage that it facilitated the assimilation of non-Russian peoples: the agents of the Tsar simply superimposed themselves on existing tribal and other personal hierarchies. The state was constructed, then, not through building institutions and promulgating laws, but by riding piggy-back on personal bonds. The clearest and most important instance of this phenomenon was serfdom, which arose during the fifteenth and sixteenth centuries, but was never properly defined in law. All the same, it persisted till the 1860s, when the Tsars embarked on the hazardous process of trying to build proper state institutions and a civil society.[3]

At the lowest level, the social tradition which cemented the system was *krugovaya poruka*, or "joint responsibility", which implied that the whole community, the *mir*, was responsible for the obligations and also the misdeeds of individuals. *Krugovaya poruka* originally arose as a means of ensuring criminal justice. It goes back to the earliest juridical documents associated with principalities of *Rus'*. Princes and their officials were unable to cope with enforcing criminal law or custom over their extensive territories, so they left it to local town and village communities to do so. If a murder or other serious crime were committed, communities had to discover and apprehend the miscreant themselves, or else pay a fine to the prince.[4] Later on, taxation was organised in the same way. For princes or even their local officials to determine

---

[2] Pipes, Richard, *Russia under the Old Regime*. Harmondsworth, Peregrine Books, 1977, pp. 64-79.

[3] LeDonne, John, *Absolutism and Ruling Class: the Formation of the Russian Political Order, 1700-1825*. New York, Oxford University Press, 1991, chapter 1; Afanas'ev, M.N., *Klientelizm i rossiyskaya gosudarstvennost'*. Moscow, Tsentr Konstitutsionnykh Issledovaniy, 1997.

[4] Dewey, Horace W., 'Russia's Debt to the Mongols in Suretyship and Collective Responsibility' in: *Comparative Studies in Society and History*, vol. 30, 1988, pp. 249-70.

the amount of tax payable by each household was too cumbersome. Instead, a total levy was imposed on each town or village community and the distribution of the burden within the community was left to its members. Similarly, when troops had to be raised for a military campaign, each community was required to raise a certain number of recruits and had to decide for itself which of its members should perform military service.

This procedure meant that vital state functions were accomplished in a personal and informal manner and that the subjects of law were communities, not individuals or even households. Each urban and rural community held meetings of all heads of households, which took the vital decisions regarding criminal proceedings, taxation and recruitment by mutual negotiation and consensus. It would also elect a *starosta* or elder, who was responsible for ensuring that decisions were carried out and for handling relations between the community and the higher authorities. For the system to survive, it was vital that each member of the community had enough to live on and a small surplus. If your neighbour's household was indigent, then you would end up having to pay part of his taxes. If your neighbour's sons were unhealthy, then it could be your sons who went off to war instead.[5]

The implications of this system were very far-reaching. It meant that all members of the community, especially the village community, had an interest in ensuring the minimal welfare of each other. If one household suffered a fire, then other villagers would rally round and help the victims rebuild their home. If one family had a serious illness during harvest-time, then other families would help them bring in the crops. This was common sense, not altruism. By the same token, many village communities would periodically redistribute land between households, to reflect family size, the capacities and needs of each family. A large family would be awarded more land, but would pay correspondingly more taxes. As a result, "mutual responsibility" became a moral as well as a juridical and administrative concept.[6]

Krugovaya poruka also meant that everyone was intensely interested in everyone else's affairs. If your neighbour drank heavily or beat his wife or had adulterous liaisons, this could weaken his family and hence his economy, to your disadvantage. Those who fell into long-term helpless poverty were unpopular, since they were a burden on their neighbours and other villagers would do their best to have them sent off to the army or convicted of a criminal offence and despatched into exile. A *starosta* had extensive powers in this regard,

[5] Burds, Jeffrey, 'The Social Control of Peasant Labour' in: Kingston-Mann, Esther and Timothy Mixter (eds.), *Peasant Economy, Culture and Politics of European Russia, 1800-1921.* Princeton University Press, 1991, pp. 52-100.

[6] Blum, Jerome, *Lord and Peasant in Russia from the Ninth to the Nineteenth Century.* New York, Atheneum, 1964, chapters 8-14; Aleksandrov, V.A., *Sel'skaya obshchina v Rossii (xviii-nachalo xix veka).* Moscow, Nauka, 1976, chapters 2-3; Gromyko, M.M., 'Sem'ya i obshchina v traditsionnoy dukhovnoy kul'ture russkikh krest'yan xviii-xix vekov' in: *Russkie: semeynyy i obshchestvennyy byt.* Moscow, Nauka, 1989, pp. 7-24.

which he might exercise according to his personal feelings. The affluent were also regarded with suspicion, since their relative wealth suggested they were acting illegally, or at least in ways which might jeopardise community solidarity. As a popular saying had it, "Poverty is a sin against the *mir*; wealth is a sin against God." Such attitudes encouraged gossip and, worse, denunciation, as villagers tried to rid themselves of burdensome or untrustworthy neighbours.[7]

So, *krugovaya poruka* generated some of the most attractive and unattractive features of Russian social life: on the one hand, the tradition of humanity, compassion and mutual aid towards one's fellow human beings, on the other, that of malicious rumour-mongering and denunciation directed against the poverty-stricken, the eccentric, sometimes even against the talented and unusual.

The modernisation of Russia from Peter the Great onwards actually *strengthened* the archaic institution of *krugovaya poruka*. Personal hierarchies and joint responsibility impeded the emergence of a modern state, a modern market economy, a civil society and a nation, all of which are mutually dependent on one another. All the same, post-Renaissance European culture did penetrate Russia from the late seventeenth century. It was deliberately imported by the tsars, in order to sustain Russia's status as a European great power. In order to live up to that status, it needed modern science and technology as well as a European-educated elite, capable of holding its own in the courts and diplomatic circles of European society. Russian aristocratic salons, academies, universities and publishing houses were powerful centres of a new kind of Russian culture, an imperial, European and largely secular culture, remote from the world of the peasants and the Orthodox Church. So there were really two kinds of Russianness, *russkiy* (ethnic) and *rossiyskiy* (imperial). The national identity of the elite was cultural and linguistic, but lacked roots in the peasantry and the church. Bridging this gap was the principal challenge which faced the great cultural figures of 19th century Russia.

Of Russia's major writers, only Dostoevsky came close to fashioning a myth which combined the imperial and the ethnic in a coherent vision. His views were set out most consistently in *"The Brothers Karamazov"* and in his journalistic writings published as *"Diary of a Writer"*. He believed that the ordinary Russian peasants and workmen were a "God-bearing people" who had preserved the customs of mutual aid long ago abandoned by more "advanced" European nations. Through their humility and their suffering, they had shaped themselves to understand other peoples and to embrace them in a peace-loving union. However, they needed the might of the imperial state, which had gathered numerous territories and peoples and organised them, together with Russians, to promote peace in the world. During the Russo-Turkish War of 1877-78 Dostoevsky hoped that the Third Rome would conquer the second, Constantinople, and inaugurate a reign of "eternal peace" in the Slav spirit.[8]

[7] Mironov, B.N., *Sotsial'naya istoriya Rossii perioda Imperii*. Vol. 1, St Petersburg, Dmitriy Bulanin, 1999, pp. 327-32; quote on p. 330.
[8] Dostoevsky, F.M., 'Dnevnik pisatelya', April 1877, in his *Polnoe sobranie sochineniy*. Vol. 25, Leningrad, Nauka, 1983, p. 100.

The Russian state was not, however, as Dostoevsky conceived it. It was not messianic and had no wish to be seen as the "Third Rome". On the contrary, it suppressed the messianic myth which had underlain earlier Russian national identity and which was still strong in the Orthodox Church and among its parishioners. That myth remained the heritage of the Old Believers, those who rejected the church reforms of the mid-17th century.[9] The tsarist state never claimed the heritage of the "Third Rome". Its justification was temporal and geo-political. Its legitimacy depended above all on the success of its armies, which from the mid-17th to the mid-19th century was very remarkable. The Tsar was crucial to its symbolism: he was commander-in-chief of the armed forces and father of his peoples, the ultimate guarantor and unifier of all those patron-client bonds.[10]

*   *   *   *

The Soviet Union, like Tsarist Russia, was a multi-ethnic empire; unlike Tsarist Russia, it *was* a messianic state. The Bolshevik form of Marxism absorbed the latent messianism of the Russian people: that was what distinguished it from Western European Marxism. (One might add that Russian messianism was supplemented in this case by Jewish messianism: the Soviet Union should probably be seen, at least initially, as a joint Russian-Jewish project.) Paradoxically, however, that messianism did not take a national form, but an extremely international one. The word "Russia" did not appear in any form in the name of the new state. Russia had no effective political existence within the Soviet Union. The Communist Party was the bearer of power and there was a Ukrainian, Georgian, Kazakh, etc. Communist Party, but no Russian Communist Party. Since the Communist Party was the focus of power and the bearer of the messianic vision, that lack was a peculiarly sensitive one. The Russian people was simply dissolved in a higher entity.

The Soviet Union did create many of the characteristics of a nation, as understood by Karl Deutsch, Ernest Gellner, Benedict Anderson and the "modernist" theories of nationalism: large industrial cities, a mass education system, a penetrative network of communications and public media, a centralised welfare system, a conscripted army. The language employed as the cement of that system was Russian, the common history and traditions evoked in schools as the shared heritage were mainly Russian. But the potential nation thus adumbrated was not Russia, it was what the leaders liked to call the "Soviet people". Nor were the Soviet leaders engaged in nation-building: they regarded national feeling as a kind of pubertal disorder, a necessary but regrettable phase in social evolution, which should be completed as rapidly as possible. Their

---

[9] Hosking, Geoffrey, *Russia: People and Empire*. pp. 64-74.
[10] Wortman, Richard, *Scenarios of Power: Myth and Ceremony in Russian Monarchy*. Vol. 2, Princeton University Press, 2000.

ultimate aim was the creation of an international proletarian community, of which the "Soviet people" were the forerunners.[11]

At another level, though, the Soviet vision *was* a Russian one. Bolshevism perpetuated elements of the inherited system of Russian myths and symbols: the idea that Russia has a special mission in the world, to practise and disseminate Truth and Justice (*Pravda*) based on egalitarianism and the way of life of ordinary toiling people. By virtue of this special mission, Russians felt themselves entitled to exercise patronage or protection over less developed people; this was a form of service to them, what one might call "the Russian's burden". Such an outlook was compatible with Soviet Communism and it constituted the practical, working ideology of many Russians employed by the Soviet state. Yet it was also close to Dostoevsky, which is why I consider him the unacknowledged "shadow ideologist" of the Soviet Union.

Soviet Communism was both Russian and anti-Russian, then. A contemporary Russian political scientist has summed up its ambivalence; "Bolshevism's exploitation of the Russian mytho-symbolic system had ambiguous consequences. On the one hand it ensured that the Communist ideology was convincing, it imparted immense dynamism to all spheres of social life and guaranteed the legitimacy of the new state and its socio-political institutions. On the other hand, the glaring contradiction between the new reality and the *ethnic* interests of Russians in the long run weakened the mobilisation potential of the Soviet mythologems and degraded the imperial mythology."[12]

In the first ten to fifteen years of the Soviet state, Russian identity was explicitly rejected and spurned. The tsarist empire was condemned as a "prison of the peoples". On his passport application form, Lenin wrote "No nationality", while Trotsky, when asked whether he was Russian or Jewish, replied "Neither; I am a Social Democrat and an internationalist." The doyen of Soviet historians, Mikhail Pokrovsky, claimed that "the term "Russian history" is a counter-revolutionary term", while Nikolay Bukharin asserted that it was necessary to discriminate *against* Russians, so that they could "purchase the trust of previously oppressed peoples".[13] Ukrainians and Belorussians, as East Slav peoples close to the Russians, were given their own separate Union Republics. *Narkomnats*, the body responsible for nationality policy, had representatives from every ethnic group *except* the Russians. Cultural and educational policies deliberately promoted non-Russian languages in the non-Russian republics: in Ukraine, for example, all primary school children were taught in Ukrainian, including Russians, Jews, Greeks etc.. "Indigenisation" (*korenizatsiya*) favoured

[11] Smith, Jeremy, *The Bolsheviks and the National Question, 1917-1923*. London, Macmillan, 1999; Martin, Terry, *The Affirmative Action Empire: Nations and Nationalism in the Soviet Union, 1923-1939*. Ithaca, Cornell University Press, 2001, chapter 1.

[12] Solovey, Valeriy, 'Russkie protiv imperii' in: *Svobodnaya mysl'*, 2002, no. 12, p. 82.

[13] Vdovin, A.I., Zorin, V.Yu. and A.V. Nikonov, *Russkiy narod v natsional'noy politike: xx vek*. Moscow, Russkiy Mir, 1998, pp. 87, 91, 109.

non-Russians for higher education and then advanced and promoted local officials to run the non-Russian republics. Non-Russians were given their own ethnically-named administrative territories, at all levels, down to the village soviet. Thus, in Ukraine there were district and even village soviets which were recognised as Jewish, Greek, Armenian, German, Polish etc. – but no Russian ones, otherwise whole large cities, like Khar'kov and Donetsk would have become Russian enclaves. The Russians were too numerous and powerful for their own good. The American historian Terry Martin has called this the most ambitious affirmative action programme in history.[14]

During the 1930s, there was something of a return to Russian symbolism. As early as 1930, Stalin reminded the poet Demian Bedniy that one could not write off all Russians. "In the past there existed two Russias, revolutionary Russia and anti-revolutionary Russia," while today's Russian working class was the most advanced in the world. In a later speech he added, "In the past we had no fatherland and could not have one. But now that we have overthrown capitalism, now that power is with us, the people, we do have a fatherland, and we shall defend its independence."[15] By the mid-1930s, though, it was not only revolutionary Russia or the working-class which was being rehabilitated, but the Tsars who had created and defended the Russian Empire and had thus, albeit unintentionally, made the Soviet Union possible. In the schools, Russian victories were once again celebrated, while Ivan the Terrible, Peter the Great and Alexander I were extolled as great leaders.[16]

We should note, though, that this rehabilitation of Russia was entirely imperial, not ethnic. It was, if you like, neo-*rossiyskiy*, not *russkiy*. On the contrary, Stalin continued energetically to pursue policies aimed at the destruction of the two most important aspects of the life of ethnic Russia: the Orthodox Church and the village commune. Parishes were being closed, church buildings sequestrated, priests arrested, imprisoned and not infrequently murdered. Peasant households were being herded into collective farms and the most productive farmers exiled to Siberia and Kazakhstan. Nor did *korenizatsiya* cease its work in favour of the non-Russian nationalities.

That was the state of affairs until the outbreak of the Second World War. In order to secure the whole-hearted support of the Russian people, the Soviet regime needed to deepen Russianization, to make it ethnic as well as imperial. That was because, contrary to the expectations of the ideologists, the war turned out to be not a class war, but a national war – soon referred to as the Great Fatherland War. It was not toiling peoples versus imperialists, but Russians versus Germans. Stalin reacted to this situation with a rehabilitation of some aspects of ethnic Russia. There was a partial return to private farming and a

[14] Martin, Terry, *o.c.*, chapter 2.
[15] Vdovin, A.I. etc, *o.c.*, pp. 125-29.
[16] Brandenberger, David, *National Bolshevism: Stalinist Mass Culture and the Formation of Modern Russian National Identity, 1931-1956*. Cambridge, Mass., Harvard University Press, 2002, chapters 3-4.

free market in agricultural products. The Russian Orthodox Church was permitted to restore the patriarchy, re-establish seminaries and reopen parishes. In the public media, there was much more emphasis on home and family life as valuable for their own sake, not just for the building of socialism.

There was more freedom in literature too and one work summed up the rehabilitation of Russian ethnic values. This was the narrative poem by Aleksandr Tvardovskiy, *"Vasiliy Terkin"*. Its hero is a simple Russian soldier from a village in Smolensk province. He has minimal education and no interest in science, technology or industry. He is completely apolitical: the text never mentions the Communist Party or even Stalin. He is proud to defend the Soviet Union which, it is implied, is simply a continuation of Russia. Altogether, Terkin is more like a figure from the imagination of nineteenth century *narodniki* than a Soviet Communist hero. Yet this was the truly popular literary work of the war, which Soviet soldiers carried in their knapsacks and read in their spare time. It marked the honourable re-emergence of the *russkiy* in what had hitherto been a *rossiyskiy-sovetskiy* cultural synthesis.[17]

During the war, then, Russianness crystallised as an amalgam of imperial and ethnic elements, partly *russkiy*, partly *rossiyskiy* and partly *sovetskiy*. Given wise leadership, the Soviet Union might have become a huge compound federated state, like modern India, with the Russians as the leading nationality, the "elder brother", as Stalin called them in a speech at the end of the war.

It was not wisely led, however. Even during the war, Stalin had slighted some aspects of national solidarity. For example, he regarded Soviet prisoners-of-war in German captivity as traitors and abandoned them to their fate, refusing to accept the mediation of the International Red Cross in keeping in touch with them or alleviating their living conditions. Before, during and after the war, his massive deportations of certain ethnic groups, including many of the Russians' East Slav brothers and sisters, the western Ukrainians and Belorussians, generated an enduring legacy of bitterness directed against both Russians and Communists. For some peoples, the prospect of a Union led by Russians or Communists became permanently unacceptable.[18]

In addition, the concessions to ethnic Russia permitted during the war were swiftly withdrawn afterwards. The collective farms were fully reinstated, with delivery targets which left the peasants poverty-stricken and demoralised. The Orthodox Church was once again downgraded and restricted: it was used as an instrument in foreign policy, but most forms of congregational religious life remained forbidden. The relative freedom tolerated in the arts was revoked, party control once again tightened and the publication of war memoirs was prohibited during Stalin's lifetime. Even the celebration of victory in the war

---

[17] On the popularity of *Vasiliy Terkin*, see Grishunin, A.L., *Tvorchestvo Tvardovskogo: v pomoshch' prepodavatelyam*. Moscow, MGU, 1998, pp. 40-45.

[18] Hosking, Geoffrey, 'The second world war and Russian national consciousness' in: *Past & Present*, no. 175, May 2002, pp. 162-87.

and mourning for the huge losses was restricted to occasions which the party could organise and monitor. Memory became part of the tightly controlled official narrative.[19] Where memory cannot be periodically reinforced by the spontaneous exchange of personal recollections in the community, it becomes insubstantial and fragmented and cannot function as a foundation of national identity. So the *sovetskiy* and the *russkiy* once again drifted apart.

Messianism remained, but it gradually changed its nature. For the first twenty years or so after the war, it was still directed towards the future, towards the building of communism. As that came to seem an ever more distant and unreal ideal, however, messianism reoriented itself towards the past. After all, even if it had not built paradise, the Soviet Union unquestionably *had* saved Europe from the apocalypse, from subjection to Nazi rule. Especially after 1964, the centre of gravity of Soviet symbolism shifted from the future to the past, to remembrance and celebration of that great and undeniable victory. Fixated on the past, Soviet spiritual life became ghostly and insubstantial and lost the power to convince young people.[20]

Another feature of old Russia reasserted itself under the Communists and obstructed the formation of a Russian national outlook. Between the 1860s and 1910s, civil society, representative institutions and even a measure of pluralist politics had been emerging. *Krugovaya poruka* was abolished in 1905. But the 1917 revolution abruptly ended that development. Russia was plunged back into unrestricted rule by persons, now intensified by the fact that it was ostensibly being exercised in the name of a messianic ideology and therefore of absolute right and wrong. Both the party and the state in theory ruled through elective institutions, but in practice the nomenklatura appointments system consolidated personal rule by, in effect, creating a monopoly system of patronage. Appointments at the highest levels in all professions were monitored by appropriate-level party committees, which collated information on personnel from party cells, trade union branches and the security police. High-level appointees became patrons who, when they were promoted, took their clients with them, in a process which one political scientist has likened to groups of mountaineers roped together making their way up a steep slope: *Seilschaften*. No alternative political parties or genuine elections existed to provide any competition.[21]

At the grass roots, *krugovaya poruka* made an unacknowledged return. The collective once again took responsibility for the individual, as well as the right to determine his identity. Urbanisation took place, but in a manner which

[19] Tumarkin, Nina, *The Living and the Dead: the Rise and Fall of the Cult of World War Two in Russia*. New York, Basic Books, 1994; Zubkova, Elena, *Russia after the War: Hopes, Illusions and Disappointments, 1945-1957* (translated and edited by Hugh Ragsdale), Armonk, NY, M.E. Sharpe, 1998.
[20] Hosking, Geoffrey, 'The Second World War'.
[21] Voslensky, Mikhail, *Nomenklatura: Anatomy of the Soviet Ruling Class*. London, Bodley Head, 1984; Rigby, T.H. and Bohdan Harasymiw (eds.), *Leadership Selection and Patron-Client Relations in the USSR and Yugoslavia*. London, Allen & Unwin, 1983.

preserved rural institutions in a new form, especially those embodying "joint responsibility". Most immigrants to the town were housed in communal apartments. Here, they reproduced the familiar features of collective decision-making, mutual responsibility and mutual surveillance backed by the authorities. The tenants shared a kind of egalitarian poverty just above subsistence level. When one tenant fell below it, others felt obliged to help out, not out of generosity or altruism, but because life alongside the destitute is stressful and contains constant potential for conflict.

This factor helps to explain why the terror of 1937-38 was so vicious: quite apart from fear and selfish considerations, many Russians felt it was their *duty* to denounce a wayward neighbour or colleague whose behaviour might weaken the collective. Besides, the members of each communal apartment elected a supervisor, who became a member of the *domovoy komitet* and through it had to maintain good relations with the janitor, with the local soviet and with the police. It was positively his (or her – they were often women) duty to report any unusual or suspicious goings-on. Similar pressures were encountered in the workplace, where each worker's performance affected the success of his work-team, or brigade, in fulfilling the output plan, and therefore the bonuses and privileges of the whole group.[22]

During the 1950s and 1960s, these forms of mutual supervision still existed, but they were no longer concentrated in the NKVD; they were institutionalised in the "comrades' courts" and the peoples' auxiliary militia (*druzhina*), which patrolled streets and apartment blocks and dealt with minor offences. As one propagandist put it, "No court is more demanding than a court of one's comrades, with whom one labours in the same workplace, shares joys and sorrows, and to whom one is suddenly revealed as not exactly the same person they trusted and thought they knew. No punishment is more effective than that imposed by a friendly hand, because it is imposed not in order to punish, but in order to help those who have made a false step to return to the right path."[23]

Anti-semitism in the late 1940s-early 1950s did much to undermine the supra-national consciousness of the ruling class, of which Russians and Jews had been the dual guarantors. Ethnic consciousness, which had begun to strengthen in the 1930s, was further intensified after the war. "Entry no. 5" (nationality) on the passport replaced social origin as the most important criterion when deciding on an individual's life-chances. Taken together with *korenizatsiya* and in the absence of state-sponsored mass terror, this meant that the non-Russian republics tended to become enclaves for the titular ethnos. The clients of the locally dominant patrons would be appointed to the top jobs,

[22] Utekhin, Il'ya, *Ocherki kommunal'nogo byta*. Moscow, OGI, 2001; Gerasimova, E.Yu., 'Sovetskaya kommunal'naya kvartira' in: *Sotsiologicheskiy zhurnal*, 1998, no. 1-2, pp. 224-42.
[23] D. Shchepakin, quoted by Kharkhordin, Oleg, *The Collective and the Individual in Russia: a Study of Practices*. Berkeley, University of California Press, 1999, p. 282.

would receive preference in the allocation of education, jobs and housing, and would also control much of the underground, "second" economy.[24]

As a result, by the 1960s or so, Russians could no longer be certain of access to favourable life-chances throughout the Soviet Union. They were no longer the unchallenged "imperial" people. They sought compensation by rehabilitating their own ethnic identity and forging their own distinctively Russian ideology. This ideology aimed at rehabilitating the values of the Russian peasant community and those of the Orthodox Church (although this aspect did not become fully clear until shortly before the end of the Soviet Union) and, at the same time, identified the de-nationalising features of Soviet rule with the Jews, or with the undue influence of "Western bourgeois ideology", thus cleansing Russian national identity of "cosmopolitanism". The leaders of the CPSU vacillated between passive toleration of this outlook, as necessary to retain the loyalty of the Russians, and suppression of it as potentially destructive for inter-ethnic solidarity.[25]

There was much for Russian nationalists to be concerned about. The pressures of the Cold War had necessitated massive rearmament and, therefore, the creation of an all-pervasive military industrial complex. Russians, together with Ukrainians and Belorussians (not distinguished from them in the non-Slav republics), became the specialist staff as well as the manual workers of that complex and of Soviet modernisation throughout the USSR. For that purpose, they migrated and settled in large numbers in the non-Slavic republics. Sometimes that migration was organised by the Soviet state, but sometimes it was spontaneous, motivated by the desire to escape rural and small-town Russia which, originally the heartland of the Russian ethnos, had by the late 1940s become one of the most poverty-stricken and demoralised regions of the Soviet Union. Rural Central Asia and the Northern Caucasus were just as poor, but less demoralised, since they tended to preserve rural communities and even some aspects of tribal and clan identity. Russians, moreover, had no national Communist Party to speak for them when the major financial decisions were being made. As the harbingers of modernisation, they deserted their own villages. In the towns, owing to cramped living conditions, uncertain health care and poor services, they tended to have few children. The Russian birth rate fell sharply, especially in relation to that in Transcaucasia and Central Asia, where the traditions of village life persisted in more vigorously.[26]

[24] Zaslavsky, Victor, *The Neo-Stalinist State: Class, Ethnicity and Consensus in Soviet Society.* Brighton, Harvester Press, 1982; Kaiser, Robert J., *The Geography of Nationalism in Russia and the USSR.* Princeton University Press, 1994, chapters 6-7.

[25] Brudny, Yitzhak, *Reinventing Russia: Russian Nationalism and the Soviet State, 1953-1991.* Cambridge, Mass., Harvard University Press, 1998.

[26] Denisova, L.N., *Ischezayushchaya derevnya Rossii: nechernozem'e v 1960-1980-ye gody.* Moscow, Institut Rossiyskoy Istorii, 1996; Senyavskiy, A.S., *Rossiyskiy gorod v 1960-1980-ye gody.* Moscow, Institut Rossiyskoy Istorii, 1995, pp. 150-81; Perevedentsev, V.I., *Naselenie SSSR: vchera, segodnya, zavtra.* Moscow, Moskovskiy Rabochiy, 1972.

Solzhenitsyn was the first to formulate clearly the burden which ethnic Russia was bearing for the sake of the Soviet universal mission. In his "Letter to the Soviet Leaders" of 1973, he lambasted the anti-national ideology which had given Russians a chronically under-productive collective agriculture, a gigantic and polluting industry and soulless modern concrete boxes for people to live in. Schools drummed empty ideological slogans into bored children, he warned, while depressed, demoralised men became drunkards and women performed degrading and unfeminine manual labour. To revive Russia's economy and her spiritual values, Solzhenitsyn argued, Russians needed to give up international responsibilities and certainly stop exporting revolution and playing a great power role in areas of the world of no interest to Russians.[27]

The experience of the late years of the Soviet Union suggests that most Russians shared some of Solzhenitsyn's ambivalence. On the whole, they were still proud of the Soviet Union, but no longer prepared to make serious sacrifices for it. As late as 1990, 70-80% of Russians regarded themselves as citizens of the Soviet Union and considered its entire territory to be their national home-land. Only 14% considered the RSFSR to be their homeland.[28] In the referendum of 17 March 1991 their ambivalence was sharply revealed: Russians voted both for continuation of the USSR and for the sovereignty of the Russian Republic.

For most of its history, then, Russia has been a multi-ethnic project defined and controlled by the state. Most Russians have regarded themselves as members of a super-ethnos which had both the right and the duty to embody a universal mission and therefore to assimilate other peoples, at least politically.[29] This vision is difficult to reconcile with a nation-state. Even Russian liberals did not intend to set up a nation-state almost until the very end of the Soviet Union; they assumed that the reforms they proposed would take effect in the Soviet Union as a whole. But they found themselves in alliance with non-Russian national movements who shared the same enemy, the autocratic Soviet state, and who wished to establish their own independent nation-states. So the logic of politics impelled them to create at least the outward forms of a Russian nation-state which few of them had envisaged or wanted.[30]

In the end, then, the decisive confrontation of August 1991 was not between Communists and anti-Communists, but between the Soviet Union and Russia or, if you like between those who still saw Russia as an empire and those who wanted a new ethnic and civic Russian nation, no longer dedicated

[27] Solzhenitsyn, Aleksandr, 'Pis'mo vozhdyam Sovetskogo Soyuza' in his *Sobranie sochineniy*, vol. 7, Moscow, Terra, 2001, pp. 60-94.

[28] *Russkie: etno-sotsiologicheskie ocherki*, Moscow, Nauka, 1992, pp. 400, 415.

[29] This was still true in the late years of the Soviet Union. See: Levada, Yu.A. *et al* (eds.), *Sovetskiy prostoy chelovek: opyt sotsial'nogo portreta na rubezhe 90-kh godov*. Moscow, 1993, pp. 13-26.

[30] Beissinger, Mark R., *Nationalist Mobilisation and the Collapse of the Soviet State*. Cambridge University Press, 2002.

to either helping or oppressing non-Russians. The outcome has been an improvised, truncated and distorted nation-state. Its legitimacy its still widely contested, especially the separation from Ukraine and Belorussia. Within it, both political and economic life are still dominated by personalities and by patron-client networks. Laws, institutions and civil society exist, but are weak and overshadowed. Most Russians are themselves discontent with what they have, so we cannot simply say that this is a Russian form of the nation-state. But whether it is developing into something else is not clear either. Russia faces the 21st century with its identity still undefined.

ON THE RUSSIANNESS OF RUSSIAN HISTORIOGRAPHY

Wim Coudenys

One of the outcomes of post-modernism is a general suspicion of historiography. Historiography, it is claimed, is either apologetic or offensive. It is always serving certain (political) goals and it is never a true representation of the past *"wie es wirklich gewesen ist"*. I won't elaborate on the epistemological problems that are raised by this general mistrust of historiography. Neither will I dwell on the moral responsibilities of the historiographer at a time when history seems to have become more popular than ever before and where history even occupies a prominent place in the world of entertainment. In Russian historiography, however, there is one issue of even greater importance than epistemological and moral considerations: the question of whether Russia has developed along similar lines to Europe, or whether it has followed its own way (*Sonderweg*). With the help of some examples, I will try to comment on this ongoing debate.

One of the striking things about Russian historiography is that its periodisation largely differs from the one that is usually adopted for Western Europe: it had no Roman period, its Middle Ages seemed darker and lasted far longer than in the West, comprising (or devouring) both Renaissance and Enlightenment; Modernity in Russia only took off with Peter the Great and existed until 1917, largely undisturbed by the earthquake of the French Revolution; and it took a brutal, Bolshevik revolution to make Russia a part of contemporary history. Russia, so to speak, continued to dwell in the *Ancien Régime* until 1917. The fall of the Romanov dynasty was considered a logical outcome of an utterly outdated political system.

Periodisation in Russian historiography is defined by the centre of power (Kiev-Moscow-St. Petersburg-Moscow), the geographic and eventually ethnic scope of its territory. It started with Kievan Rus' (*Kievskaya Rus'*), covering the period of the earliest written sources until the end of the 12th century and the arrival of the Mongols. From the 14th century onwards, Moscow gradually emerged as the new centre and gave birth to Muscovy (*Moskovskaya Rus'*). It definitely took advantage of the waning of Kievan Rus'; it profited from its isolation in the northeast and especially from the *modus vivendi* it had reached with the Mongols. Finally, in 1722, Peter the Great moved his capital from Moscow to St. Petersburg, which symbolised the new imperial state. The more or less mono-ethnic Rus' (cf. *Russkiy* still refers to ethnic Russians) gave way to the multi-ethnic concept of *Rossiya* and *Rossiyskaya Imperia* (cf. *Rossiyanin* as inhabitant of the Russian Empire). Notwithstanding the interruption of the Soviet era (which was called the *Sovetskaya Imperia*), this multi-ethnic concept has been maintained until this day (*Rossiya/Rossiyskaya Federaciya*), with the Russians (*Russkie!*) as only one of the many ethnicities. This is, of course, theoretically speaking, since the Russians remained the controlling (and thriving) force within the Russian Federation.

As such, these differences in chronology should not strike us as remarkable, especially since the larger part of world history cannot be grasped by Western standards either, let alone be compared with what happened in the West. Nor would it attract our attention at all, if there had not been that strong tendency, both in Russia and the West, to include Russia in Western historiography. Although it is generally accepted that Russia's history is quite different from Europe's, few people would agree to abandon this approach. The question is: why is this so?

Unlike the European tradition of liberal, democratic and constitutional institutions, Russia has developed a political and cultural system of its own, usually called despotic or even tyrannical, depending on the defining instance. This *Sonderweg* is either inherent to Russia, or the result of a failed historical development. Liberal-minded Russian historians of the 19th century have attributed this failure to the Mongol or Tatar Yoke, which lasted from the 13th to the 15th century. They either deplored this evolution or gave it a positive turn: it had saved the Russian empire from the drawbacks of modernity.[1] Soviet historians thought along the same lines. They were largely indebted to their liberal teachers, strongly believing the European myth of progress and were limited by their own theoretical premises, which stated that Marxism was only conceivable in a European-like state. Hence, the need to insist on state-formation and feudalism from the earliest times, as in Western Europe.[2] And there's the rub: sources on early Russian history are so scarce and largely of an archaeological type, i.e. non-verbal, so that the gaps had to be and have indeed been filled with lots of fantasy and imagination.

Before I turn to this particular trait of Russian historiography, I would first like to comment on a major dispute about the origins of Russian despotism which, at first sight, seems to best capture the spirit of Russia. In 1986, Harvard Professor Edward L. Keenan published an article on the *"Muscovite Political Folkways"*, which has become the founding charter of much modern Western writing on pre-Petrine Russia.[3] Keenan launched the idea that Russian despotism (about which he had not the least doubt) could be explained with the help of the so-called deprivation hypothesis: "the absence of Western feudal institutions of vassalage, Roman law, development of private property, primogeniture, political pluralism, corporate estates, parliamentary rule and a strong church to counterbalance state power."[4] Richard Pipes developed this idea even further, from a liberal and legalistic point of view. According to Pipes, Russia's missing bourgeoisie was the cause of Russia's "deviation from the

[1] Langer, L., 'The 'Strangeness' of Rus' in the Mongol Era: Problems of Comparative History' in: *Russian History. Histoire russe*, no. 28, 2001, p. 283.

[2] Poe, M., 'The Truth about Muscovy' in: *Kritika*, no. 3, 2002, pp. 473-75.

[3] Keenan, E.L., 'Muscovite Political Folkways' in: *Russian Review*, no. 45, 1986, pp. 115-81.

[4] Langer, L., *o.c.*, p. 274.

political patterns of Western Europe, and of the failure of liberal ideas significantly to influence its political institutions and practices. [...] it is reasonable to assume a more than casual connection between the notorious underdevelopment in Russia of legality and personal freedom and the impotence or apathy of its middle class."[5] Based on the sociological concepts of Max Weber, both Keenan and Pipes considered Muscovy a patrimonial regime, with a tsar ruling over his country as over a household, as if it were his private property. Unlike Western European feudalism, which gave birth to the juridical system as we know it today, a patrimonial regime would necessarily lead to a bureaucratic state. Weber's model, however, was a somewhat ideal one, largely based on the assumption that Western mediaeval society as a whole had developed along the lines set out by Weber's contemporary, the Belgian mediaevalist Henri Pirenne. More recently, it has become evident that in reality European mediaeval culture did not correspond to Pirenne's models: not all cities were centres of international trade that had successfully contested the power of the sovereign ruler; primogeniture was not the custom throughout Europe, on the contrary; even the suggested relationship between feudalism, legality, freedom and prosperity is at the very least questionable. So, when questioning this tyranny of typologies, it becomes clear that the Russian mediaeval city, albeit less and later developed than many of its European counterparts, does not necessarily constitute an exception to the European rule. However, to go from there to saying that Russian mediaeval cities were identical to European ones, is also an exaggeration. Russian cities bore *some* resemblance to Western cities, but were much smaller, more self-sustaining and less defended; moreover, they came into existence with a delay of some 100-150 years. The harsh climate, the remoteness and distances, as well as a less well-developed economic and ultimately backward agrarian system, not to mention, of course, the plague and other (natural) disasters, are plausible explanations for this.[6]

However, Russian historians continue to claim that Russia had reached the same level of development in the early Middle Ages as the West. They eagerly compare the Russian *veche* to the western City Councils, although the *veche* did not have the same power and fairly soon ceased to exist altogether. Moreover, not unlike their colleagues in the West, Russian historians turn a blind eye to the fact that economic development and the rise of personal freedom are not necessarily linked to each other and they keep repeating that the arrival of the Mongols in the 13th century meant that Russia could no longer develop along the lines of Western history.[7]

Some scholars have now explicitly addressed the problem of whether Muscovy's origins were Byzantine or Mongol. If the latter is true, it could explain why Muscovy had turned to (presumed oriental) despotism. It is often claimed that Russian bureaucracy, associated with despotism, has a Mongol background. These claims are usually based on the fact that administrative functions in

[5] Pipes, R., *Russia under the Old Regime*. London, 1974, p. 191.
[6] Langer, L., *o.c.*, pp. 280-88.
[7] *Ibid.*, p. 283.

Muscovy, especially those referring to tax collection, had indeed been of Tatar origin. On the other hand, the Mongols did not actively interfere with Muscovite administrative practices, which in reality remained to a large extent the same as those that had existed before the Tatar invasion. "Though there may be certain affinities between Muscovite and Mongol administrative practice, there are also many parallels with medieval household government common in Western Europe. [...] a medieval household system of governing that was framed by traditional Kievan practices, but which from the fourteenth century became more systematised – a process not unlike the emergence of the *Chambre des Comptes* in fourteenth-century France."[8] Once again, the conclusion seems to be that there are far more affinities between Russia and the West, or for that matter between Western European and Byzantine practices, which leaves the question of the origins of Russian despotism unanswered.

Contemporary Russian historiography, however, suffers to a large extent from what I would call the tyranny of "conceptualisation". The particularity of Russian history is reduced to "local circumstances" and embedded in a more typological, even universal approach to historiography. This problem has been tackled by the American historian Marshal Poe, who accuses Keenan and his kind of purposely neglecting accounts of Western travel to Russia that bear witness to the despotic rule in Muscovy.[9] According to Poe, this omission is partly due to the political correctness of the 1970s and 1980s (Détente, support for Gorbachev's perestroika) and the negative image of pre-Petrine Russia, created by 19th century Russian historians. Poe turns to Aristotle to formulate an alternative: Muscovy's rule was indeed despotic, but not tyrannical; if that had been the case, according to Aristotle, the people who were suffering from it would have overthrown such a regime. In this respect, Poe has no (moral) problem in calling Muscovy a despotic country, especially as it has, in the style of Aristotle, a positive ring to it. Poe's approach helps us accept that Russia indeed went its *Sonderweg*: it is corroborated by Western travel tales; it accounts for the fact that Russia bore little or no resemblance to the European feudal society with its restrictions on absolute power; it explains why there were no political bodies representing the people and "that the various sub-units of the Muscovite State were created by the crown and existed solely at its pleasure." As such, Russians did not believe "they had a firm 'right' to defend their persons or possessions before the crown."[10] To explain the existence of despotism (not tyranny!) in Russia, Poe turns to the traditional arguments: the harsh climatological conditions, necessitating a struggle for survival; the popular and wide-spread Biblical concept that life on earth is only a punishment for original sin (hence the futility of resistance); the Greek or Byzantine political concept that rulers are appointed by God; the ignorance of Renaissance political thinking. Poe concludes optimistically that Russia was a poor and primitive country that was permanently under siege but which, unlike other northern states, had

---

[8] *Ibid.*, p. 291.

[9] Poe, M., *o.c.*, pp. 473-86.

[10] *Ibid.*, p. 482.

managed to survive.[11] This proved the effectiveness of the despotic system, notwithstanding its moral drawbacks.

There is no doubt, however, that Poe's conclusions also suffer from political correctness, in as much as he calls the Russian *Sonderweg* "successful" in its own way and does not explain why Russian despotism would be better than any tyranny. Above all, it is not obvious why his approach would be less dogmatic, for instance, than that of the Harvard school he is criticizing.[12] In my view, another American scholar, Charles Halperin, comes closer to the truth, when he criticises the concept of "Muscovy as a Hypertrophic State."[13]

Halperin departs from the observation that 19th century Russian historians believed that in Russia, the State had produced a Society, rather than that Society had been the source for the emergence of the State, as was the case in Europe. This was best defined by the Russian historian Klyuchevskiy, who wrote that the *sosloviya* (estates, classes) were "defined by their obligations, not their rights."[14] Halperin has grave doubts about the correctness of this hypothesis and produces three strong objections:

Firstly, historiography tends to be synchronic rather than diachronic. What period of Muscovite history are historians talking about? The 16th century can hardly be compared to the 17th century, especially when we take into account that the political upheaval and socio-cultural changes during this period were only rivalled by those of the revolutionary era around 1917. Ivan IV (the Terrible), who ruled during the second part of the 16th century (and is therefore a contemporary of the Spanish King Philip II and not some obscure tyrant from the darkest Middle Ages) served during the 17th century as an example of how tsars should NOT govern their country. How then can you call Ivan the Terrible, who cruelly oppressed his subjects during the *Oprichnina*, "typical", when even in his own age his reign was considered a distortion?

Secondly, Russian historiography is largely based on theory, not on practice. In theory there were no limits to the power or arbitrariness of the tsar – practice shows, however, that the autocrat was limited by the (admittedly) unwritten obligations he had towards his subjects: their loyalty in turn was based on the assumption that they would be treated honestly by the tsar; demands that could not reasonably be met led to uprisings and political turmoil (this was particularly the case in the 17th and 18th centuries). A tsar, for instance, could not unrestrainedly conscript soldiers or raise taxes! One can even wonder about the efficiency of the tsar's power, given the poor condition of the

---

[11] See his recent *The Russian Moment in World History*. Princeton, 2003.

[12] Kivelson, V.A., 'On Words, Sources, and Historical Method: Which Truth about Muscovy?' in: *Kritika*, no. 3, 2002, pp. 487-99.

[13] Halperin, C.J., 'Muscovy as a Hypertrophic State: A Critique' in: *Kritika*, no. 3, 2002, pp. 501-07.

[14] Klyuchevskiy, V.O., *Istoriya soslovii v Rossii*. 1887; cit. in Halperin, C.J., *o.c.*, p. 502.

communication and transportation systems and the general lack of technology in Russia. (One should not forget that the industrial revolution in Russia only started at the end of the 19th century!) The existence of autonomous social spheres, where the tsar had little or no direct control (e.g. Siberia, the borderlands (Cossacks)) did not imply the approval by the tsar, but existed through sheer necessity.

And thirdly, Russian historiography is based on a kind of abstraction and does not take reality into account. Historiographers have focussed on the role of the State, but have consequently neglected the role of individuals in the process of state-formation. As an example, Halperin refers to the tendency among the nobility to free themselves from their duties toward the tsar/state, without losing their lands and properties (originally granted in exchange for these duties). This tendency is totally overlooked in historiography, which pretends it was in the State's interest to free the nobility, whereas it actually responded to a demand from the nobility.

Halperin argues that the idea of Russia as hypertrophic state clearly reflects the interests and ideals of liberal Russian historians who dominated historiography at the turn of the 19th and 20th centuries. The historians of that period wanted to explain why Russia had not developed along the same lines as Western Europe and blamed the hypertrophic state for that. Halperin has serious doubts about this analysis: "Simply put a *potential* hypertrophic state, a hypertrophic state *manqué*, a 'wannabe' hypertrophic state, a hypertrophic state 'in theory' cannot have dominated society the same way as an *actual* hypertrophic state [would have done]."[15]

I am well aware that Halperin is referring explicitly to the question of Russia as a hypertrophic state as such, but I am also convinced that his criticism is applicable to Russian historiography as a whole. In a volume on Russia in the Arnold Series *"Inventing the Nation"*, Vera Tolz develops the idea that historiography has largely contributed to Russia's national identity and self-perception.[16] As in many other countries, (serious) Russian historiography had its roots in the Age of Enlightenment, which was brought to Russia in the 18th century. This introduction took place at a time when Russia's rulers - Peter the Great and his successors (the majority of them women) - radically replaced the mediaeval traditions of Muscovy with Western culture. The ultimate symbol for this transition was the city of St. Petersburg, which was conceived 300 years ago as a window on the West. As a result of this, the West, i.e. Europe, and especially the comparison between Russia and the West, became the major if not sole issue in the emerging intellectual debate. One could even wonder whether there would have been an intellectual debate at all in Russia if there had not been that political turn to the West. Russians, of course, had been aware of the West before the 18th century. As early as the 16th and especially 17th

---

[15] Halperin, C. J., *o.c.*, p. 507.
[16] Tolz, V., *Russia*. London-New York, 2001.

centuries, the West was considered evil, but then almost exclusively in a religious sense. If I may make a little aside, I would say that the animosity between Russia and Ukraine is largely based on this religious perception of the West. After the emergence of Muscovy in the 13th and 14th centuries, the territory of what was once Kievan Rus' came under Lithuanian and eventually Polish control. Ukraine was integrated into Muscovy only in 1652 but, by that time, the Theological Academy of Kiev had adopted some Catholic theological ideas. These ideas urged the Patriarch of Moscow to reconsider some of the liturgical practices that had been taken for granted in Muscovy for centuries, but that in reality had deviated from the original Greek practices. This led to a schism within the Russian Orthodox Church. I am not going to elaborate on this schism, but I can say that it caused a struggle between modern and mediaeval thinking.[17] As a result, Ukrainian was associated with Catholicism and Modernity, whereas Muscovy was believed to have preserved the mediaeval virtues. Until this day, Russians call Ukraine "Little Russia" and even deny that Kievan Rus', which Russians consider the source of their culture, has anything to do with Ukraine.

Back to the main story now. When Russia emerged from its Middle Ages and entered the modern era around 1700, the question of the relationship between Russia and the West was elevated to a higher, more general level: the ruthlessness by which the reforms had been introduced by Peter the Great and his successors seemed "mediaeval" and were completely at odds with the enlightened contents of these reforms; the reforms were aimed at replacing the tsar by the State as the source of legitimacy for Russia's existence, an ideological shift for which Russian society was not yet prepared; the Russian people wondered whether the reforms had not been the work of an Antichrist (Peter the Great) from which only foreigners, Westerners, benefited. Key positions in trade, the administration, the army and the newly founded academia were indeed occupied by foreigners and, worse still, even the Russian throne fell to foreigners. The worst or best example, if you like, is definitely that of Catherine the Great, who was a German Princess and did not have a drop of Russian blood in her veins.

Whatever the case, all this provided plenty of material for the intellectual debate that emerged in the second half of the 18th century. One of the main issues in this debate was the origins of Russia. Two German historians at the Russian Academy of Sciences, Gotlieb Bayer and Gerhard Müller, advanced the idea the Varangians or Vikings, i.e. people of Germanic origins, had been the first princes of Rus'. This so-called Norman theory had two underlying ideas that upset the Russians, namely that the "Russian State" was relatively new and that it had been founded by foreigners. A huge scandal erupted when, on the day commemorating Empress Elisabeth's name day, 6 September 1749, Müller delivered a speech on the *"Origins of the Russian People and their Name"*, repeating the main points of the Norman theory. The story about the Eastern Slavs calling on the Varangians (Vikings) to come and create their state was to

---

[17] See: Scheidegger, G., *Endzeit. Russland am Ende des 17. Jahrhunderts*. Bern-Berlin etc., 1999.

be found in the *Primary Chronicle.* These facts were equally known to the Russian members of the Academy, but they had argued that the *"Rus'"*, i.e. the Varangians, were an Eastern Slavic tribe. Müller's identification of *"Rus'"* with the Varangians was considered blasphemous (especially since Peter the Great had defeated Sweden) and as an attempt to deny the originality of the Russians. To this day, many Russians contest the Norman theory whereas, in the West it is generally accepted. Even the fact that the Normans did not subject the Slavs and quickly assimilated Slav culture cannot convince the Russians. The debate had far-reaching consequences: almost every historical discussion that followed was reduced to the question of Russia's originality and the role foreigners played in it. In the early 19th century, for instance, a manuscript was discovered, or rather had miraculously survived the great fire of Moscow in 1812. The *"Igor' Tale"* related a minor (military) event of 1185, but its importance lay in the political message it brought: Russians should unite against the enemy, while the literary quality of the *Tale* proved that Russian culture in the 12th century had reached a standard equal to or even higher than in the West. The *Tale* serves as a major source for historiographers of the 12th century, who either neglect or take for granted the unintelligible passages in the *Tale.* There is not one Russian mediaevalist or historian of early Russian culture who has not written about the *Tale* and in 1995 a five-volume encyclopaedia of the *Igor' Tale* appeared. Although there have been doubts about the authenticity of the *Tale* since the very beginning, it has only recently been proved a forgery. But, since it was an American scholar (Edward L. Keenan) who proved this, it is unlikely that this proof will soon be accepted in Russia.[18]

The intellectual debate of the 19th century between Westernisers and Slavophiles began with the same question: how original could Russian culture and history be? In extreme cases, Russian culture could either be rejected (e.g. the most extremist adherents of the 1825 Decembrist mutiny/uprising) or idealised (e.g. Dostoevsky's Russian messianism), but generally the participants in the discussions agreed that Russia had indeed developed along a particular path and that the time had now come to take full advantage of this. The general idea was that the Russian peasant had remained untouched by Western culture and had thus preserved some positive characteristics that had been lost in the West (and for that matter in the Westernised upper-classes of Russia). Hence the idea that the decadent West could be saved by Russia. Not unlike the Slavophiles, whose image of old Russia in which the peasant was loyal to the tsar served as the symbol of Russianness, the Westerniser Aleksandr Gertsen saw (non-Marxist, populist) socialism as the Russian national philosophy. Like the Slavophiles, he believed that Russia's backwardness was an asset and he was convinced that it would ultimately make Russia the example for both East and West. Contrary to the traditional Slavophiles (or for that matter the classical

---

[18] Keenan, E.L., 'Was Yaroslav of Halych Really Shooting Sultans in 1185?' in: Gitelman, Z., L. Hajda, J.-P. Himka,and R. Solchanyk (eds.), *Cultures and Nations of Central and Eastern Europe. Essays in Honor of Roman Szporluk.* Boston, 1998, pp. 313-27; Keenan, E.L., *Josef Dobrovský and the Origins of the 'Igor Tale'*, Dumbarton Oaks Public Lecture, December 9, 1998.

Westernisers), Gertsen's view had a tremendous impact on what was to come. Not only did his views coincide with what the silent, peasant majority in Russia believed to be the truth, they also seem to have smoothed the way for the Bolsheviks.

The Bolsheviks presented Russian socialism as an alternative to the capitalist world. Contrary to the internationalism the Bolsheviks were spreading among Western communists through the Comintern and related organisations, the policy of Soviet Russia itself - the Soviet Union as of 1922 - remained utterly nationalistic and entirely based on the antagonism between Russia and the West. Soon after the revolution, the Bolsheviks got rid of the modernist culture that had initially accompanied their movement (the poet Vladimir Mayakovsky committed suicide in 1930) and embraced the "classics" of Russian culture, including 19th century historiography. They not only surpassed their tsarist predecessors in despotism/tyranny, but also exceeded them in applying the traditional Russian (pre-Petrine) symbols to their rule. They moved the capital back from St. Petersburg to Moscow, replaced icons with the portraits of Lenin and laid the foundations for a personal cult which bore a huge resemblance to that of the pre-Petrine tsars; Bolshevik slogans like "If a man will not work, he shall not eat" were directly derived from the Bible (in this case St. Paul's Second Epistle to the Thessalonians). Attempts to write a true Marxist history of Russia, in which these nationalistic traits were neglected, ended with the daring historians being prosecuted and condemned. In the end, the interests of the Soviet Union totally coincided with those of Old Russia.[19]

These facts, however, have been interpreted in several ways, both by historians and non-historians. Historians have a tendency to make an abstraction of the phenomena they observe and have trouble incorporating items that do not corroborate their theses. The interpretation of Bolshevik rule in Russia, for instance, is one such item. Initially, the seizure of power by the Bolsheviks was understood as a radical rupture between past and present: the Bolsheviks would turn Russia into an advanced European state. Soon, it became clear that there was virtually no rupture and that Bolshevism was little more than "socialismus asiaticus" or the implementation of Russian socialism. This observation gave birth to a whole series of historical studies, in which the true character of Bolshevism - Western or typically Russian, if not oriental - was discussed. The contradictory behaviour of Stalin - at one time destroying the Old Russian culture (churches, the remodelling of Moscow) and usurping it (his affinity with historical "Russian heroes" such as Aleksandr Nevsky or Dimitry Donskoy).[20] Contemporary historians (and political pundits!) have turned to theories of nationalism and state formation in an attempt to grasp the essence of Russia. They have recycled the old idea of Russia as a failed nation with a hypertrophic state to explain how Russia differed from Western European nation-states and therefore necessarily had to develop in its own way.[21] At the same time, this

[19] Tolz, V., *o.c.*, pp. 69-115.

[20] *Ibid.*, pp. 105-11.

[21] *Ibid.*, pp. 3-18.

approach helps these historians to take into account the high "unpredictability" of the historic events in Russia. Russians themselves are confused about their identity, have a weakly developed sense of nationality (despite the endless efforts of the Russian and Soviet empires to impose such a feeling), do not know how to choose between Russia (or the East) and the West. This ambiguity is not confined to Russians within the Russian borders. Russians who fled their country after the Russian revolution were equally confused: they failed to produce an intelligible definition of Bolshevism and therefore could never formulate an appropriate answer to it.[22] On the one hand, it was believed that Stalinism had some definite assets for Russia's development: the Young Russian movement, for instance, believed that Stalin was defending Russia's national interests and hoped that a reconciliation between Monarchism and Bolshevism would be possible.[23] The Eurasians in turn believed that Soviet Russia was not a Western or Asian state, but an Eurasian Empire and therefore became eager Soviet spies.[24] On the other hand, the majority of the *émigrés* remained irreconcilable with the Bolsheviks. Faced with potential allies in the West (including Nazi Germany), they presented the Bolsheviks as mediaeval tyrants who had brought down the Russian (Europeanised) Empire and were now threatening the West. In private, however, many *émigrés* believed that they were the sole preservers of Russian culture and they firmly opposed every attempt to besmirch Russia's historical reputation.[25] So, when Prince Saltykov published an article in 1938 on the contribution of foreigners to Russia's development, he was severely criticised for propagating the Norman theory![26] Many *émigrés* believed in the Protocols of the Sages of Zion, a fraudulent plan for Jewish world domination (probably) fabricated by the tsarist secret service in the early 20th century. They were convinced that the Bolshevik revolution was the first stage in the execution of this plan and they provided Hitler and his likes with the arguments for seeking a final solution.[27] After the Second World War, a Russian *émigré* in San Francisco announced the discovery of a proto-Slavic text that "proved" that the Russians - or their ancestors - had had a highly developed culture long before the West. Although the text is definitely a forgery, it still enjoys remarkable popularity among Russian nationalists.[28] You have only to

[22] See: Burbank, J., *Intelligentsia and Revolution. Russian Views of Bolshevism 1917-1922*. New York-Oxford, 1986.

[23] Massip, M., *La vérité est fille du temps. Alexandre Kasem-Beg et l'émigration russe en Occident*. Chêne-Bourg, 1999.

[24] Kiselev, A.F. (Ed.), *Politicheskaya istoriya russkoy migratsii 1920-1940 gg. Dokumenty i materialy*. Moskva, 1999, pp. 236-302.

[25] Raev, M., *Rossiya za rubezhom. Istoriya kul'tury russkoy migratsii 1919-1939*. Moskva, 1994, pp. 124-51.

[26] Soltykoff A., 'Le Secret de la Russie. (Essai de psychologie collective)' in: *Revue catholique des Idées et des Faits*. 3.12.1937, pp. 6-8; 10.12.1937, pp. 6-8; 17.12.1937, pp. 17-22.

[27] Burtsev, V.L., *V pogone za provokatorov. Protokoly Sionskich Mudretsov. Dokazannyy podlog*. Moskva, 1991; cf. Vetter, M., 'Die russische Emigration und ihre 'Judenfrage'' in: Schlögel K. (Ed.), *Russische Emigration in Deutschland 1918 bis 1941. Leben im europäischen Bürgerkrieg*. Berlin, 1995, pp. 109-24.

[28] Tvorogov, O.V., 'Vlesova kniga' in: *Trudy otdela drevnerusskoy literatury XLIII*. Leningrad, 1990, pp. 185-224.

watch the Russian Internet to see how the uniqueness of Russia - especially in comparison with the West - is cultivated. Obvious frauds or history writing entirely corrupted by the Europe-Russia dichotomy will not stop them from wishful thinking.

It is now time to return to the central theme of this article, i.e. the Russianness of Russian historiography. It must be clear by now that Russian historiography is based on a framework of set stereotypes, determined by the comparison between Russia and the West. It may well be Russia's tragedy that historians have failed to surpass this determinism and, even worse, that they have facilitated if not inspired the tragic development of Russian history. The question remains, of course, of whether there is any way to end this deadlock. A popular solution nowadays is analysis of the historiographic discourse. I am referring again here to Vera Tolz, who argues fairly convincingly that the Russia-Europe dichotomy has dominated Russian history writing since the early 18th century, which in turn had an important impact on Russia's political, military and socio-cultural behaviour. Russian historiographers have purposely selected their arguments from scarce early Russian and mediaeval sources, to suggest in this way a unique Russian tradition throughout the whole of Russian history. However, a theory that took shape in the 18th century may have influenced the self-perception of the Russians throughout subsequent centuries, but cannot readily explain why Russian tsars, princes, etc., behaved as they did, why Kievan Rus' and Muscovy developed as they did. Before the 18th century, perhaps the 17th century, competition with the West was hardly an issue. If I may be allowed to make a suggestion - and I am well aware that I am not a mediaevalist, so please excuse me – I would say that opportunism is at the heart of Russian history. This, for instance, would explain why the Muscovite rulers - tsars as of the 15th century - collaborated with the Tatars (who in turn helped them to get rid of their competitors) and contested the Tatar authority, only when it had practically vanished. At the same time, it might explain the often-unpredictable behaviour of Russia, or the frustrating ease with which it switches allies. But this, I suppose, should be the subject of another debate.

FEDERALISM AND ADMINISTRATIVE REFORM BY PRESIDENT PUTIN IN THE CONTEXT OF DEMOCRATIC TRANSITION IN RUSSIA

Irina M.Busygina

In Russia as in the other countries in transition which have chosen federative order for organizing political relations between the centre and the regions, federalism represents a special and very important dimension of transition. Moreover, at the same time, federalism has significant influence on all the other dimensions of transition – in other words all reforms should proceed from the fact that they are taking place within a *federation*.

The new era in the shaping of Russia's statehood definitively began with the new President, Vladimir Putin. This concerns in the first place the sphere of federative relations. Today we are witnessing a crucial change from their previous development. Thus, two tasks seem to have predominant importance: firstly, to appraise the achievements of the "Eltsin period" in developing federalism in Russia and to show how these achievements correlate with the general process of democratic transition in the country and, secondly, to investigate the meaning of the administrative reform of the new President, again putting it into the context of the democratisation process. "No political actors in Russia have a clear perception of where to move, by what rules to play and which goals to achieve," wrote V. Ryzhkov, the famous Russian politician and the deputy of Russia's Federal Assembly, recently describing the period of the "latest Eltsin".[1] The basic idea of President Putin, known for his pragmatic views, is to build a strong, and at the same time "effective federal state".[2] How do these two ideas correspond with each other? What were his first steps on this path? And how should we assess them in the context of democratic transition after three years?

---

[1] According to Ryzhkov, political actors include people of Russia, the President, the Government, the Federal Assembly (State Duma and the Federation Council) and Russia's regions. See: Ryzhkov, V., *The Fourth Republic: Essay on Political History of Contemporary Russia.* Moscow, 2000, p. 115.

[2] See: Remington, Thomas F., 'Russia and the "Strong State" Ideal' in: *East European Constitutional Review,* Vol. 9, no. 1/2, Winter/Spring 2000.

Basic Features of the "Eltsin Federation"[3]

Federal order in Russia, in my opinion, was built in the beginning of the 1990s by "unconscious design".[4] It was definitely designed in an artificial way since its main institutions were constructed "from above"; they did not grow out of existing political practices. However, this design was unconscious because the real functioning of these institutions and the rules of the game were determined not by a systemic approach and a clear vision of strategic goals, but primarily by concrete political momentum (as our politicians would argue, "proceeding from political advisability").

First of all, let us look at the main stages of building federative relations in the Russian Federation. I would stress that, at the beginning of the 1990s, prior to the new Constitution, the slogans of federalism served as a cover (and justification) for spontaneous and hence uncontrolled decentralisation, i.e. the process by which the constituent entities (regions) misappropriated functions and competences from the federal bodies of power. Over several years (the period of "democratic activism") President Eltsin tried to balance the interests of the regions and those of the federal centre,[5] making serious concessions to the regions.

The Federal Treaty of March 1992 did not change the situation. However, it diminished the threat of territorial disintegration of the country. Besides that, according to the Treaty, all regions received the status of constituent entities (subjects of the federation).[6] At the same time, the document established the asymmetric character of the federation, since its subjects were divided into four types: (1) republics; (2) kraya, oblasti and the cities of federal subordination; (3) autonomous districts and (4) an autonomous oblast'. In this complicated system, the republics were endowed with more rights and competences than the other regions.

In 1993, when political crises in Russia had been solved by anti-constitutional means, the federal centre (in this case the President) increased its influence. On 12 December 1993 the new Constitution was adopted by referendum. This document has seriously strengthened the institute of the Presidency in Russia and laid the foundations for federative relations in the country. However, it did not solve some existing urgent problems. I will mention two of them.

---

[3] I make a clear distinction between *federalism* as a set of political ideas and the *federation* as an existing state order.

[4] This paper does not examine the "pseudo-federalism" of the Soviet period.

[5] At the beginning of the 1990s there was no one federal centre, it was deeply split, so in this context I mean the President and the government.

[6] In the Constitution of 1977, only ethnic republics were listed as the subjects of the federation (RSFSR).

Firstly, Art. 5 of the Constitution declares the principle of equal status for all subjects; at the same time, some other articles of the Constitution stress that their status is not equal. Hence, the text of the Constitution is contradictory *per se*, generating permanent tensions between republics and the other regions.

A second essential problem, which was not resolved by the Constitution, is the so called "matryoshka paradox", referring to the fact that seven subjects of the federation (kraya and oblasti) contain nine other subjects (autonomous districts). The Constitution evades the problem by granting the subjects the right to find a solution themselves in Art. 66. So far, the Constitutional Court has also been unable to find a convenient solution.

At the next stage of development, bilateral (or intrafederal) treaties were signed between the Federation and its subjects, concerning the delimitation of the competences between federal and regional bodies of the state power. Initially, the idea was to sign such treaties only with the most "difficult" regions: Tatarstan, the Chechen Republic and Kaliningrad Oblast' (because of its exclave geographic location). Thus, the treaties were designed to have an exclusive character. The first treaty was signed with Tatarstan in February 1994; it contained serious contradictions with the Federal Constitution.[7] In July 1994 the Kremlin established a special commission responsible for the preparation of the treaties. Meanwhile, the process lost its initial "exclusive" logic: nowadays such treaties are signed with 48 regions.

What role did these bilateral treaties play for federative relations in Russia? In different sources, I found a whole range of evaluations: from extremely negative (the treaties as an "absolute evil") to quite positive. The opponents of this practice stress their serious objections to the Constitution of the RF and the *de facto* transformation of the constitutional federation to a contractual one. The proponents, on the other hand, believe that these documents contributed to reducing the tensions between the federation and its regions and, moreover, correspond to the nature of the federation in Russia, making it more flexible. I would not overestimate the role of the treaties. First of all, massive contradictions with the Constitution were registered only in the first two treaties (with Tatarstan and Bashkortostan). Secondly, these documents were signed only by heads of federal and regional executive powers, they were not ratified by the federal and regional legislatures. The discussions on these treaties as political institutions, that were recently rather heated, gradually became marginal and currently have no relevance at all.

Having briefly mentioned the main stages of the federative process in Russia, let us now formulate the most essential features of the "Eltsin federation". I would like to stress here that, at that time, Russia was definitively a federation *de jure*, if we determine the latter as a constitutional system in which the competences are shared between the central and regional

---

[7] It was stated there in particular that Tatarstan was not a constituent entity of the Russian Federation, but was associated with it.

governments and where regions have special or entrenched representation in the decision-making procedures at federal level.[8]

Firstly, in spite of the fact that federal relations in Russia were to some extent shaped in institutions and legislation, they remained unstable and lacked clear mechanisms. Instability manifested itself in three main aspects: (1) the extremely complicated structure of the federation and its asymmetric character; (2) the gigantic disproportions between the regions in terms of regional *per capita* product, size of the territory, population numbers and economic profile;[9] and (3) the weakness of the federal centre, which before 1999 had almost totally lost its capacity to influence the situation in the regions. The policy of the federal centre towards the regions was generally an *ad hoc* policy determined by short-term factors of a political, economic, ethnic or even (and often) personal character. The Eltsin federation thus had "weak legs": its transformation into a more centralised union or loose confederation was only a question of time.

Secondly, President Eltsin tried to build his relations with the regions on a system of exclusivity, political favouritism and personal bargaining. Informal institutions and rules of the game either began to replace new formal institutions or to fill an existing institutional vacuum.

Thirdly and perhaps most importantly, federalism in Russia did not acquire the value of a public good, it was still federalism "from above", something to be designed depending on the political situation. Not only does the population not treasure the federation, it does not understand the sense and need for federalism. Yes, William Riker wrote that federalism was a "rational bargain" between political elites,[10] but Daniel Elazar stressed that federalism was something more than a structural construction, it was a special mode of political and social behaviour, including commitment to partnership and active cooperation from individuals and institutions.[11] In other words, federalism defends private interest and at the same time proceeds from it. The people of Russia lack this self-interest in federalism.

The "Eltsin Federation" and Democratic Transition.

From the very beginning of the 1990s, the democratic public in Russia has been discussing the predetermination of a federalist future for the country.[12] Federalism was seen as the most suitable way to strengthen the democratic qualities of the new political system. The famous phrase of Thomas Jefferson

---

[8] See, for example: King, P., *Federalism and Federation*. London, Croom Helm, 1982.

[9] Let us compare, for example, Moscow and Kalmykia: they are not on different levels of socio-economic development, but at different historical stages!

[10] Riker, William, *Federalism: Origin, Operation, Significance*. Boston, Little Brown, 1964.

[11] Elazar, Daniel, *Exploring Federalism*. Tuscaloosa, University of Alabama Press, 1987, p. 479.

[12] For more details about these discussions, see: Kamenskaya, G., *Federalism: Mythology and Political Practice*. Moscow, 1998, pp. 96-109.

"Federalism is the territorial form of democracy," was very popular as a quotation in articles and much loved by democratic intellectuals. They took this phrase for granted, as a guiding principle. Later, Jefferson's phrase was "creatively" developed and experts as well as politicians started to say: "Federalism is imperative for a democratic Russia," or "Such a huge country cannot become democratic and civilised, being based on unitary statehood [...] There is no [...] future for Russia without federalism."[13] Federalism was considered the most successful direction for the democratic reforms in general.

Thus, we have prescribed federalism for ourselves just as, in a way, we prescribed democracy. Moreover, we have strictly bound these two concepts: he who believes in Russia's democratic future should also believe in federalism - and *vice versa*. The condition and speed of development of federative relations were considered "thermometers" of Russia's democratic transition in general. Such a strict link between federalism and democratisation proved to be an essential mistake and political practices proved this, destroying the myths created by romantically oriented democrats. What were these myths? First of all, the idea that federalism with its checks and balances system would prevent the misuse of power in the regions. On the contrary, the abuse of power and the violation of human rights in the regions have massively increased. In most of the regions, consolidation of the political regimes has proceeded not on a democratic but rather on an authoritarian basis: political scientists started to use the term "feudalisation".[14] Thus, in Russia, federalism did not strengthen the openness of the society and did not increase the transparency of the political system; rather, on the contrary, it has led to a situation where the regional level was separated from the federal level while the latter was also separated from the system of local self-government.

At the same time, the hope that federalism would lead to an increase in civil activity and to the development of a participation culture and of structures of civil society was not justified. As a general conclusion, I have to state that the federalism that we have built in Russia either did not contribute to democratisation in the regions, or did so only to a very limited extent. This sad situation stimulated a new mood in society – from enthusiasm to disappointment in a federalism that "did not fulfil its promises" (which, by the way, it never made). The need for reforms became obvious. Various versions of federative reform – from constitutional to administrative – were discussed in academic circles. The reality proved to be more clean and simple: reform of the federation was and is now being realised by President Putin and his team.

---

[13] Lysenko, V., *From Tatarstan to Chechnya. Shaping of the New Russian Federalism*. Moscow, 1995, p. 16.

[14] This means fragmentation of the political space and consolidation in the regions' political regimes of personal power, which has the goal of monopolizing administrative and financial resources.

Administrative Reform under President Putin

The reforms under President Putin have several aspects and include a whole package of documents. The main elements of the reform are the following:

- the creation of seven federal districts and the nomination of the Presidential Representatives there;
- the institution of federal intervention;
- the reform of the Federation Council;
- the reform of the system of local self-government;
- the harmonisation of legislation.

Let us examine briefly each of these elements and their possible consequences for federative relations and democracy in Russia.

The Federal Districts

The Presidential Decree on seven federal districts, as a first step towards reform, initially created positive reactions in the regions. Such a Decree was almost expected by the experts since the idea of federal districts was not new and had circulated within the Presidential Administration since 1994. Later, when the governors in the regions were not nominated but elected and the "power vertical" had been destroyed, discussions became more active. Moreover, it became obvious that the previous institution of the Representative of the President in the regions had become outdated and that attempts to put new substance into old "skin" would not work. Initially, the Representative of the President in a region was regarded by Kremlin politicians as a figure, having practically the same political weight as the governor. However, even in 1995 it became clear that in most of the regions the Representative was totally suppressed by the governor. The Representatives should but could not play an independent role in the regional political scene; in Stavropol Kray for example, the Representative simultaneously held the position of vice-governor of this region.

Another problem occurred: the coordination between various federal agencies working in a region was very weak and often depended on regional executive power; they were *de facto* "privatised" by it.[15] In many regions, federal structures acted not in the interests of the federal centre, but in the interests of regional establishment.[16] Thus, the Decree represents an attempt to separate federal agencies in the regions from regional executive power and to increase the presence of the President in the regions. President Putin has broken with the previous tradition, where President Eltsin's support in the regions was built on personal loyalty from the governors and personalised relations with him. Putin creates new institutions between the President and the governors.

---

[15] These are regional agencies of the Ministry of Foreign Affairs, the Tax Service, the Tax Police, the Ministry of Interior, Ministry of Defence, etc: over 380,000 people.

[16] See Smirnyagin, Leonid, 'Wonderful Seven' in: *Russian Regional Bulletin*, 2/10, May 2000, p. 22.

How this system will work is not yet clear: the competences of the representatives are written in the Decree in a rather general way, so the practical work and political weight of the representative will depend mainly on their personal qualities. They will have to work under conditions of resistance (direct or more indirect) from the regional elites. The Presidential Administration is now creating the new regulations on the competences of the Representatives of the President which should correct all the shortcomings of the previous document: to strengthen the link between the Representatives and the Presidential Administration and to widen their possibilities for influencing the regional economic sphere.[17] Hence, the Representatives should not only coordinate but also determine the economic development of the regions.

According to consultations, the Representatives see their place in the districts in quite different ways; so far they have not elaborated any common position on their role in the political or economic processes. I would accept the position of S. Kirienko, the Representative of the President in the Privolzhskiy Federal District, as the most reasonable. He does not consider the Representatives as independent actors in the political process, but as instruments for the "inventarisation of the country", meaning careful calculation not only of natural resources and productive infrastructure but, above all, human capital, level and quality of education, schools of thought and cultural legacy. Another idea sounds quite important in my opinion: the history of this institution should not and will not be the history of personal successes or failures: the Representatives will either succeed or fail together, as a new institution.[18]

As for the experts and analysts, one can find some very polarised considerations concerning the meaning of the new institution. Some are inclined to examine it very seriously, as a "unitarian superstructure over the federation,"[19] while the others see it as "pure technological rationalisation."[20] I would not overestimate this political innovation: it is directed towards a new organisation of the federal agencies in the regions but does not seek to reform (at least formally) the system of the state power in general.

Finally, analysts often stress and perceive as quite dangerous the fact that the Federal Districts correspond to the military ones and that five out of the seven representatives are generals. It seems to me that this looks rather logical if we take into account the personal sympathies of the President and the details of his *curriculum vitae*. He would probably like to nominate all seven generals as his Representatives if it would not provoke too strong a reaction from public opinion. It is also worth mentioning that not a single republican capital has been chosen as the centre of a Federal District.

---

[17] *Vremya Novostey*, November 16, 2000.

[18] *Nezavisimaya Gazeta*, October 25,.2000.

[19] See: Zubov, A.B., 'Unitarianism or Federalism (To the Question of the Future Organisation of Russia's State Expanse)' in: *POLIS*, 2000, no. 5, p. 32.

[20] See: Kaspe, S., 'To Construct a Federation – *Renovatio Imperii* as a Method of Social Engineering' in: *POLIS*, 2000, no. 5, p. 67.

The Institution of Federal Intervention

The shaping of this institution has been accomplished by the Federal Law "On the changing of the Federal Law 'On general principles of organisation of legislative and executive bodies of state power of the subjects of the Russian Federation", adopted by the State Duma, 19 July 2000. The initial Federal Law had been adopted by the Duma only in October 1999. It had extreme significance for the regions, but had been stopped for years – first by the President, later by the Federation Council.

As a result, the law was adopted too late: the regions had already adopted their constitutions and statutes and regional political regimes had been consolidated. Under such conditions, the Federal Law could only record the situation in the regions: the dominant position of the executive power (governor or president) and the possibility of part-time work for regional deputies (they could combine their deputy mandates with business or work in municipal bodies). Nor did the law foresee the institution of federal intervention and responsibility of the regional bodies. In other words, the Law of October 1999 is the best argument for the thesis that at the end of the Eltsin period the federal centre had practically no mechanisms for influencing the situation in the regions.

The new Federal Law of 19 July 2000 had to improve the situation. It tries to close the "gaps" in the previous law, in envisaging the following:
- the responsibility of the regional state power bodies for violation of the federal Constitution and federal legislation;
- the possibility for the President to dismiss regional legislature (if the Duma approved);
- the possibility of dismissing, by Presidential Decree, the head of the executive power of a region, issuing a law or legal act contradicting the federal Constitution or federal legislation;
- the possibility for the President to dismiss the head of the executive power of a region accused by the General Prosecutor.

In fact, the institution of federal intervention is a normal phenomenon that corresponds closely to the federal order (see for example, in Germany, the so-called *Bundeszwang*). The law in general (as well as in Federal Districts) increases the presence of the federal centre in the regions and decreases the status of the governors, changing drastically the whole logic of the development of the previous period. In this respect, I consider the political will of the President to be legitimate, in order to prevent further consolidation of authoritarian regional political regimes which could also prosper due to the weakness of civil society structures in the regions.

Reform of the Federation Council

The Federation Council or, as it is called in Russia, the "collective voice of the regions" happens to be a rather peculiar institution. During its short history, the principle of the formation of this institution has been changed three times.[21] Thus, in December 1993 the deputies of this body were elected directly by the population (two from every subject); in 1995, after long discussions, the principle was changed and the heads of the regional legislative and executive branches of power received their mandates without elections. Finally, in July 2000, the Federal Law was adopted according to which the Federal Council is formed from two representatives from each subject of the federation – one representative from the legislative branch, being elected by regional deputies, and one representative from the executive branch, nominated by the governor (on condition that there is no vote against this candidate by two thirds of the legislature).

In the context of this study, I probably should not examine in detail the place of the Federation Council in Russia's political system. However, it should be said that since 1995 the Federation Council has shown a lot of pragmatism, being oriented on consensus rather than on confrontation with the President. V. Ryzhkov calls this body a "political stabiliser."[22] In addition, the Federation Council turned out to be a kind of political school for regional leaders and the basis from which they could move to the national level.

Hence, the question arises of whether the reform was really necessary. In general, the proponents of the reform use the following arguments:
- the deputies of the Council work on a non-permanent basis, so the technical apparatus of the body is much too big and costly;
- half of the deputies are heads of the regional *executive* power, although in the Council they should perform *legislative* functions;
- finally, the Council does not represent Russia's regions, but its regional elites.

These arguments seem to me fairly well substantiated. The principle adopted in 1995 was definitely not ideal and reform was needed. But what kind of reform? I believe that the best way of forming the Federation Council would be by direct elections of the deputies in the regions (as was done in 1993). Such a suggestion was made by Elena Mizulina, the deputy of the State Duma from the Yabloko faction, but did not gain support. It is a matter of principal importance that in the Federation Council the regions should be represented by some alternative figures and not by the regional leaders or their representatives.[23]

In Russia, however, a different principle that seems to me rather dubious has been chosen. Firstly, the new Federation Council, being composed of regional representatives, would not correspond to the constitutional competences of

---

[21] Art. 95 of the Constitution does not exactly foresee the principle of the formation of the Federation Council.

[22] See: Ryzhkov, V., *o.c.*, pp. 98-99.

[23] See: Busygina, Irina, 'Federation Council in Russia's Political System' in: *Russian Regional Bulletin*, no. 2, February 1999, pp. 8-10.

this body since these deputies have no political weight nor do they act under their own name on Russia's political scene. Thus, the new principle means a weakening of parliamentarianism in Russia, decreasing the parliament's role in the system of the division of power. Secondly, the new principle *per se* shows clearly the very meaning of reform, that is to push the governors away from the Council and to take away their immunity as deputies. In this context, the reform is undertaken with the same logic as the introduction of the institution of federal intervention.

The first implications of this innovation are already visible. We observe not only an atomisation of the Federation Council, but also its transformation into a lobbying body. The deputies have become political managers employed by regional executive and legislative bodies: the governor can easily dismiss his political employees.

Reform of the Local Self-Government System

The reform of the local self-government system has been undertaken through the Federal Law "On changing the Federal Law 'On general principles of organisation of local self-government in the Russian Federation," adopted by the State Duma, 7 July 2000. The law foresees a new procedure: the possibility of dissolving the representative body of local self-government as well as dismissing the heads of municipalities if they issue a legal act contradicting the Federal Constitution, federal or regional legislation. The representative body can be dissolved by a regional or federal law, while the head of a municipality can be dismissed by a decree of the governor or by Presidential Decree.

This federal law is obviously the weakest and most dangerous element of the whole reform system. It is well known that in spite of permanent declarations about its primary importance, local self-government in Russia is characterised by dependency on the regional executive power, extremely low financial possibilities and low public support. The Federal Law works not in favour of but counter to the development of the system of authentic self-government in the country, placing it *de facto* within the system of the state power as its lowest level; this is contrary to the Federal Constitution. In fact, one could speak of the compensational character of the law: the federal centre (in this case the President) introduces an institution of federal intervention, enabling him to dismiss governors; by way of compensation the governors are given the comparable possibility of dismissing heads of municipalities. It is a conceptual mistake since, according to the Constitution, the bodies of self-government are principally different from the nature of state power.

This article does not seek to analyze the problems of local self-government in Russia in detail. It is important to mention, however, that these two directions of reform (federalism and self-government) should not be analyzed separately, but only in terms of their relationship. The newest political developments, in particular the project suggested by the so called "Kozak Commission", show that the very character of reform (it ignores Russia's territorial diversity) corresponds to the re-centralisation of the Federation launched by President Putin.

Harmonisation of Legislation

This element of administrative reform was not introduced by a special law, but the two federal laws that we have already discussed contain statements according to which all previously adopted regional legislation should correspond to the Constitution and federal laws, while the legal acts of local self-government should correspond to federal and regional legislation.

The problem of contradictions in the legislation at different levels is not new. This has been actively discussed for several years now, as massive contradictions became one of the basic characteristics of the Russian Federation. The scale of contradictions is enormous, so the political will of the federal centre in this direction looks quite justified. Basically, V. Putin began his efforts in this field quite some time ago: several days after his inauguration, he sent letters to the parliaments of Bashkortostan and Tatarstan, in which he prescribed placing the Constitution and republican laws in relation to the Constitution of the Russian Federation (not to the bilateral Treaties, as was stressed by the President) and federal laws.[24] The special commission working in Bashkortostan since the beginning of February 2000, has already found 350 contradictions.[25] President Putin has decided to begin with the republics which, in their legislative base, have accumulated the most contradictions with federal legislation (paradoxically, the Republic of Dagestan, one of the most politically loyal to the federal centre republics, contains in its legislation the largest number of contradictions to federal laws of any of the republics of the Northern Caucasus).

In the other regions, the legal evaluation was launched as one of the first activities of the Representatives of the President. For example, in the Ural federal district the evaluation has discovered that approximately one sixth of regional legal acts does not correspond to federal legislation.[26] In August 2000 S. Kirienko signed an agreement with the governors of the regions comprising Privolzhskiy Federal District, that by the end of 2000 all regional legal acts should be brought into conformity with federal legislation.[27] In spite of the quite unrealistic timetable, the intention was positive.

The working process has started, but it has an uneven character. Some regions (for example, Moscow) directly or indirectly resist administrative pressure from the centre. The head of the Constitutional Court of the Republic of Bashkortostan has declared that not all contradictions should be corrected

---

[24] Remington, Thomas F., *o.c.*, pp. 102-3.

[25] *Nezavisimaya Gazeta*, October 10, 2000.

[26] Busygina, Irina, *o.c.*, pp. 3-4.

[27] *Nezavisimaya Gazeta*, August 30, 2000.

(in the first place those regulating economic development). He argues that there is no mechanism of interaction between regional and federal parliaments: the State Council (Parliament) of Bashkortostan has sent some 4000 suggestions correcting federal legislation to the State Duma (at the discussion stage) but none of them has been examined.[28] Other regional leaders also argue that some federal laws are certainly far from perfect.

Looking briefly at the elements of Putin's administrative reform, let us summarise in table form the main features of the Eltsin and Putin federations:

Features	Eltsin	Putin
1. Character of relations with the regions	exclusive, political favouritism	"equalisation"
2. Support of the President in the regions	governors	Representatives in federal districts
3. Institution of federal interference	no	yes
4. Political status of the governors	high	low
5. Political Status of the Federation Council	(rel.) high	(rel.) low, shared with State Council
6. Formal/Informal Institutions	mainly informal	mainly formal
7. Responsibility of regional/ local authorities	no	yes

Regional Reactions to the Reform and Compensation from the Federal Centre

In general, the reactions of the regional leaders to the reform package of President Putin were positive. This came as a big surprise to the experts and mass media. Most of the regional leaders have quietly accepted the new institution of the Federal Districts and the Federation Council deputies have voted for the new principle for shaping the Council. Only two regional leaders declared their clear disagreement with the new decisions. E. Rossel', the governor of Sverdlovsk Oblast', famous for his attempt to conduct independent political and economic policy, spoke against excessive competences for the Representatives as well as against the budgetary policy of the federal centre. However, his resistance has been suppressed by the Representative P. Latyshev and E. Rossel' has declared these objections "misunderstandings".[29] The President of Chuvashiya, N. Fedorov, tried to organise resistance to the President in the Federation Council and even launched an appeal by the deputies to the Constitutional Court, but failed; the deputies decided not to take the risk.

---

[28] *Nezavisimaya Gazeta*, October 7, 2000.
[29] *Nezavisimaya Gazeta*, November 1, 2000.

However, he was the only one who published articles in the central mass media in Moscow containing clear criticisms of the presidential reforms.[30] Most of the regional leaders preferred to keep silence or to discuss the reform carefully: only within their regions with confidential persons and only the elements they like (for example, new competences for the regional executives regarding local self-government). It also should be stressed that the reform (in particular the Federal Districts) gave new opportunities to regional business elites to gain access to new markets.

Thus, surprisingly, we have to state that no regional opposition has been expressed in Russia. These local battles with the President or his Representatives, attempted in the Federation Council or by certain regional leaders, were undertaken not for victory but in order to obtain the best conditions of surrender and to receive more compensation from the federal centre. I see three lines of such compensation for regional leaders.

The first and most important: the creation of the new body – the State Council. The President was repeating everywhere that this should be a "political body of strategic importance." The scale of the problems discussed within the Presidium of the Council[31] would shock the imagination: strategic planning,[32] hymn and heraldic, etc.. Since the Council has only advisory status (and this is the key word), the scale of the matters discussed by it is not that important. President Eltsin, acting within his competences, created an advisory Presidential Council, composed of the "most wise and respectful" people in the country, the political weight of which was zero or close to zero. President Putin, acting also within his competences, has decided to create another advisory body in order to compensate the governors for the loss of their political status. The magazine *Itogy* has called the Council "the factory of governor's dreams"[33] and I suspect this is close to reflecting the truth.

The second form of compensation is the Law "On the third period" that the President promised to M. Shaymiev, the President of Tatarstan. The meaning of the law, which is an amendment to the Federal Law "On general principles of organisation of state power in the Subjects of the Russian Federation" is that one should count the period of the competences of a President or governor only from 16 October 1999, the date when this law came into force. Hence, more than 20 regional leaders have been given the possibility of being elected for a third time.

---

[30] See: Fedorov, N., 'On Dictatorship and Law' in: *Nezavisimaya Gazeta*, October 25, 2000.

[31] The Presidium of the State Council is composed of seven governors nominated by V. Putin, one from each Federal District. They will be replaced according to a rotation principle.

[32] At the first session, V. Ishaev, the governor of the Chabarovsk kray, presented a report "The Strategy of the Development of the State to 2010." The discussion of this report would not be appropriate in this paper, but one of the conclusions of the report, pointing out the need to adopt a special federal law on federal relations, seems very dubious to me: all the basics of Russia's federative statehood are laid in the Federal Constitution.

[33] *Itogy*, November 28, 2000.

The third form of compensation is connected with the Federation Council. The deputies managed to postpone the introduction of the law on the new principle of its formation for one year, as it was stipulated to come into force only on 1 January 2002. This corresponded perfectly with the personal interests of the deputies since, for many of them, their period of office would be over and at least some of them hoped to stay in Moscow, probably as a member of the new Federation Council. The law favoured this hope.

Some Conclusions

In general, the institutional federative system in the Russian Federation has been shaped under President Eltsin. The system not only inherited some drawbacks from the Soviet period, but also developed in a distorted way during the 1990s. Therefore, the reform of Russian federalism was badly needed.

In discussing the nature of the reforms, I can state the following. The reforms have now acquired an irreversible nature. The legislative shaping of the reforms has been carried out extremely quickly. This became typical of Russia's reforms in general since we tend to "save" Russia in the first instance and therefore do not always have the time to evaluate the consequences of our reforms. Imbalanced as it is, the institutional system allows for such rapid movements. Pushed by the President and his team, the reform has an aggressive nature. It became possible thanks to the unique political situation in recent years: no confrontation between the President and the Parliament (as the role of the latter as independent actor in the political process has obviously declined). The reform has not been discussed in society, it was undertaken by administrative pressure. In other words, the President did not feel the necessity to discuss his intentions with society, while society accepts such an attitude rather indifferently.

The reform is not constitutional but administrative in nature. However, it is clear that the administrative field happened to be rather wide: it proved possible to achieve a great deal without affecting the Constitution. The reform preserves the institutions, but changes their substance, their interaction and the rules of the game. The reform shows that, even if the superficial forms of the institutions are there in Russia, their functioning and political weight can still be the object of political experimentation.

It would be quite difficult and probably counter-productive to evaluate the reform in positive or negative terms. As I have tried to show, it contains neutral (probably, positive in context), dubious and negative (reform of local self-government) elements. However, the basic sense of the whole reform is not more centralisation, but destruction of the system of federative relations built up under President Eltsin. The previous model of centre-periphery relations should be changed drastically according to the reform. It was discovered that the previous system did not have supporters: neither political parties, regional elites or society in general are eager to defend the Eltsin

Federation. The experts now tend to write that "we have to abandon gradually the kind of federalism that is unsuitable for Russia," that "federalism as organisational principle for Russia's political space does not have a solid historical foundation,"[34] etc..

The character of the reform reflects in particular President Putin's vision of federalism, the nature of which he believes consists of "strengthening the power vertical." In this vision, federalism is perceived as a set of technological operations that touch the delimitation of competences between federal and regional power levels, but does not penetrate society. The reform seeks more formalisation regarding the functioning of the institutions but, paradoxically, it has occasionally already lead to the opposite - more "un-formalisation" (the Federation Council is a good example).

One of the strategic goals of the reform is to weaken the regional elites (especially the governors)[35] and to concentrate resources (administrative and financial) in the hands of the federal bureaucracy. Regional elites and oligarchs have left the federal political scene. But this was only part of the task. The other part lies ahead: the federal bureaucracy should become a driving force, providing economic growth at any price. So the Eltsin Federation has been sacrificed to the task of economic growth and administrative reform should not be examined *per se*, but in the first place as a means to create a framework for economic growth.

The next conclusion results from the previous one. If we take the goal of economic growth for Russia at any price, values such as democratisation, open society, federalism (those which were at least articulated during the Eltsin era), necessarily recede into the background. Democracy risks becoming a victim of the ideas of the strong state and order. Indifferent (and in some cases positive) reactions from society to such transformations show that, after ten years of reforms, these values are still not perceived as being for the public good by Russian society.

The model of federalism can only be national, it should correspond to national statehood in general. As a political principle, it is a product of national statehood and its development. Evaluating the meaning and results on the level of federalism, we should proceed from this perspective.

[34] See: Zubov, A.B., *o.c.*, p. 54; Kaspe, S., *o.c.*, p. 55.
[35] The President stressed that "there were, are and will be no special relations between the Kremlin and the governors" in: *Nezavisimaya Gazeta*, September 29, 2000.

POLICY, LOYALTY AND GEOGRAPHIC CONSTRAINTS IN RUSSIA[1]

John Löwenhardt

Does Russia today have the political system that allows it to deal effectively with its economic and social problems? In order to answer this question I should briefly deal first with the economic and social problems that require government action. What are these? They can of course be analysed in various ways, the crucial question being what criteria one wishes to use to assess the current situation in Russia. I believe it is obvious that Western criteria are not particularly useful. Better perhaps to apply Russian criteria, to ask Russians themselves. The best criteria are people's own standards. People evaluate their situation in the light of their own recent history. Without much exaggeration, one can say that before Gorbachev started his reforms, most Russians led a perfectly "normal" life. They were then thrown into the turmoil of transition. Many lost their jobs and many lost their savings, two or three times over.

In a survey representative of the entire population of Russia in January 2000, we asked respondents how much time they thought it would take to reach a normal standard of living.[2] "Normal" standard of living was not qualified. What was to be normal was left to the individual, perhaps semi-conscious interpretation of each respondent while answering the question.

Chart 1: Time to reach normal standard of living

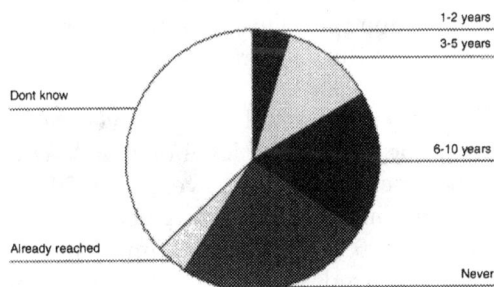

As we can see from Chart 1, the largest group of respondents simply could not answer: 37% were at a loss. One in four said a normal standard of living would never happen. Almost 18% thought it would take 6 to 10 years; 16.5% thought it would be 5 years or less, and 4% said a "normal" situation had already been reached.

---

[1] An earlier version of this paper was presented as lecture at the Institute for International and European Policy, University of Leuven on 12 March 2003.

[3] National survey commissioned by the ESRC-sponsored 'Outsiders' project in Russia (Russian Centre for the Study of Public Opinion VTsIOM) 19 – 29 January 2000; N=1,940, population 16+.

At the time of this survey, Russians had endured eight years of transition. The distribution of their answers reflects the impact of transition that is all too well-known. A small group has benefited, some of them having become extremely rich. For them, their current standard of living is normal. But a very large group, over sixty per cent, is at a loss. These are the disoriented and the pessimists. These are people who are either dumbstruck by this simple question or (25%) who say they will never experience a normal standard of living. These are the losers of transition, mainly the elderly and middle-aged, many of whom live in utter poverty or barely survive on the products of their garden plot. The rest one could call optimists, the young generation that has adapted fairly well to life in the market.

These data indicate that the outlook of the largest section of the population is gloomy. They tell very little about the causes. The most basic of these, I would say, are two, and they both concern the environment of economic life: the natural and the political environment. By natural environment I mean geography and climate; I will return to this later. In the political environment, the most essential is the failure of the Russian state so far to provide an environment conducive to investment in infrastructure and in manufacturing.

Since the crisis of 1998, the Russian economy has shown moderate growth rates, due to the partial replacement of imports by domestic production. In 2002, the economy grew by 4.2%, surprisingly somewhat more than the government had predicted at the beginning of the year. For the fourth consecutive year the state budget was in surplus.[3] For 2003 as well, the European Bank of Reconstruction and Development expects a rate of growth of some 4%. But this growth has not changed the scale of the underlying problem, that of a lack of funds to upgrade the country's antiquated assets. Economic growth in Russia has been and still is due almost exclusively to high world prices for oil, gas and metals, which remain Russia's prime exports.

At the time of the survey, annual capital investment in the Russian economy was less than one fifth of the level of 1990.[4] The average age of industrial equipment had increased from 8.5 years in 1970 to 14 years in 1995. The percentage of such equipment less than five years old had dropped from almost 4% in 1970 to less than 10% in 1996. At the time of the survey, economists estimated that Russia required about 50 billion euro per year for the modernisation of its capital stock. Another indication is the funds spent on industrial research and development. The norm in economically advanced nations is 2 to 2.5% of GDP. In Russia R&D spending dropped from 1% in 1991 to 0.32% in 1997. Russia's GDP in 2000 was half that of the Netherlands. Its foreign trade turnover was similar in value to that of Denmark, with exports

[3] Chinyaeva, Elena, 'The Russian Economy, Lost in the Dark' in: *Russia and Eurasia Review* (internet edition), 4 February 2003.

[4] This and other data from Lynch, Allen C., 'Roots of Russia's Economic Dilemmas: Liberal Economics and Illiberal Geography' in: *Europe-Asia Studies*, Vol. 54, Issue 1, Jan. 2002, pp. 31-49.

almost entirely dominated by oil and gas, with virtually no value-added products. Recently, investments in Russia have been rising slightly, but Western companies still invest twice as much in Poland as they do in Russia.[5]

The failure of the state is the root cause of Russia's problems. There is little to no disagreement on this among observers both inside and outside the country. Invariably they point to the same ills: there have been high levels of political uncertainty, resulting in high political risk for investors; the legal environment is, after many years, still inadequate, some say volatile; the regulatory system is extremely burdensome and opaque; taxation is often excessive, corruption widespread; and, last but not least, corporate governance still leaves much room for improvement.

Wealthy Russians are estimated to hold several hundred billion dollars in foreign bank accounts, thus testifying to their lack of confidence in their own state. What about those who do not have money stashed away abroad, what do they think? In our January 2000 survey we also asked how much time they thought would be needed for their government to solve the economic problems. The results are shown in Chart 2.

Chart 2: Time needed for governmt to solve economic problems

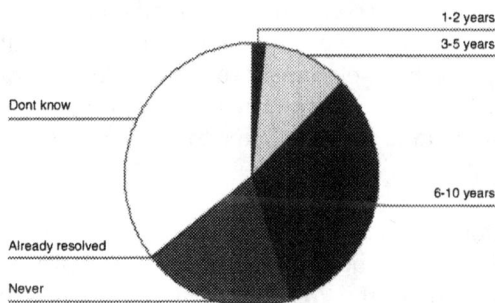

Only one in eight thought it would be five years or less. Almost a third thought it would take six to ten years, more than one third could not give a reply, while 19% thought the country would never solve its problems. Russians voiced these expectations only three weeks after Vladimir Putin had taken over the Presidency from Boris Eltsin. And it was indeed a positive sign that, a few months later, Putin asked his people not to have any illusions. He said that it would take at least fifteen consecutive years of growth at 8% *per annum* for Russia to attain the *per capita* income level of Portugal at that moment.

Since then, Putin has pushed the reform of the state – albeit not in the direction of Western-type liberal democracies. He knows as well as we do that

[5] Menkiszak, Marek, '"Prozachodni zwrot" v polityce zagranicznej Rosji: przyczyny, konsekwencje, perspektywy', Centre for Eastern Studies, Warsaw, September 2002, p. 24.

Russians are not democrats. Or, more precisely, that only very few Russian citizens have a democratic frame of mind. The Austrian researcher Christian Haerpfer has recently shown how far removed Russian society is from that of countries more to the West. On the basis of more than 53,000 face-to-face interviews in twelve post-communist countries during the period 1991-98, he has grouped populations by their score on an index of democracy.[6] Some of these countries are now "consolidated democracies" because the vast majority of their populations are democratically minded post-Communist citizens. Examples include Poland, the Czech Republic and Hungary. Others, such as Romania, Croatia, Bulgaria and Estonia, have been categorised by Haerpfer as "emerging democracies" since, there, a small majority of citizens are democrats. But in Russia and Ukraine, Lithuania and Latvia, democracy is very weak in terms of support from their own citizens. These are still "transforming societies". In the Ukraine and Russia, less than 20% of the population can be termed "democrats" by the same criteria as in the other countries. Haerpfer: "In these countries, the transformation to non-democratic regimes is not impossible and the outcome of political transformations, even ten years after the end of Communism, does not clearly indicate democracy…"Democracy"appears to be only one option of political change, which is challenged by non-democratic alternatives."[7]

How democratic can one expect a state to be if its citizens hardly support democracy? It is true that Russia's Constitution, as adopted over ten years ago, had a democratic structure. But constitutions, after their adoption, are "dressed" by legislation and the practice of political rule. Russia's constitutional history over the past decade has been extremely turbulent. And, to put it mildly, the behaviour of Boris Eltsin has not contributed to the population's confidence in democracy. But it would take too much time to go into the sordid details. So let us focus on Putin.

I will merely touch on his main reform measures. Briefly, these are the following. The parliament has been brought under control. Opposition parties and politicians still exist, but the President now has a solid bloc of support in the State Duma. The other house, the Federation Council, has been reformed and made into an ineffective collection of non-political deputies. The influence of regional governors and presidents, that had grown out of proportion during Eltsin's rule, has also been pushed back. Not only are they no longer in the Federation Council, but a new administrative layer has been inserted between them and the Presidential Administration, that of the Federal Districts.

So much for the main structures. But what holds them together? No longer the ideals of the past and certainly not the inner convictions of democracy. What holds them together these days, the governing principle so to speak, is

[6] Haerpfer, Christian W., *Democracy and Enlargement in Post-Communist Europe. The Democratisation of the General Public in fifteen Central and Eastern European Countries, 1991-1998*. London & New York, Routledge, 2002.
[7] Haerpfer, Christian W., *o.c.*, pp. 142-3.

that of loyalty – loyalty to the President. Conscious of the crucial role in politics and in television electioneering, Putin has succeeded in silencing critical channels without entirely eliminating freedom of the press. He has also made some progress in regaining some initiative for the state at the expense of the handful of influential oligarchs who dominated Eltsin's rule. The President now demands loyalty from business and financial elites but allows these to operate more or less independently provided they show loyalty when demanded.[8]

Let me now finally turn to the second basic cause of Russia's ills, one that is often overlooked: space and climate. The country's core geographic data cannot be changed. This means that, even under the best of conditions, the costs of production in Russia will be higher than almost anywhere else. The climate is the most severe in the world when measured by the contrast between the length and coldness of its winters and the brevity and heat of summers. Since 1991, this has been exacerbated by the disintegration of the USSR, because the centre of gravity of the state has shifted north by some three degrees. Due to the uneven distribution of population (Europe) and natural resources (Siberia), distance itself in Russia is a production cost not to be sneezed at. Proper road maintenance is comparatively extremely expensive due to soil conditions. In Russia, land transport tends to be five times as expensive as water transport, but the possibilities for water transport are very limited. As a result, in the mid-1990s even with average wages comparatively very low, average costs of production in Russia were 2.8 times higher than in Japan and 2.7 times higher than in the US.[9] The conclusion of Allen Lynch is simply this: on strictly liberal market grounds, most of the Russian economy should be declared bankrupt. "Russia as a whole cannot be developed economically without the state."[10] The country needs an interventionist state policy to compensate for its disadvantaged position in terms of economic geography.

So does Russia today have a political system that allows it to deal effectively with its economic and social problems? Like other countries in the region, Russia is still caught in the "orthodox paradox" of requiring a very strong state that can at the same time withdraw from economic life to allow marketisation *and* at the right moment provide leadership for institutional reform and economic policy.[11] This is a very difficult task for the leaders of a *strong* state, and an impossible task for leaders of the weak state that Russia has been over the past decade. We only need to look at China, where the decision was made to tread very carefully and slowly in the area of political reform and where economic development has been quite successful. We are indeed

[8] See: Paszyc, Ewa and Iwona Wilniewska, 'Big Business in the Russian Economy and Politics under Putin's Rule', Centre for Eastern Studies, Warsaw, CES Studies No. 5, May 2002, at www.osw.waw.pl/en/epub (retrieved 30.01.2003).

[9] Lynch, Allen C., *o.c.*, p. 39.

[10] *Ibid.*, p. 45.

[11] On the 'orthodox paradox' see: Elster, Jon, Claus Offe and Ulrich K. Preuss, *Institutional Design in Post-communist Societies*. Cambridge, Cambridge University Press, 1998, pp. 160-1.

reminded of the controversies during the Gorbachev period over how to temporise reform.

The second term in office of Russia's previous president was entirely lost time. Although one can say that, at the end of that term, Eltsin did his country at least one favour in selecting Vladimir Putin to be his successor. The two words characterising Putin's first term have been *realism* and *reform*. Very much still remains to be desired, but structural reform is at least underway. However, the instrument of reform has been a distinct militarisation of commercial and political leadership. Colonel Putin has sought to strengthen the state by saturating it with military personnel. During the period 1998-2002, the share of military personnel in the civilian political elite multiplied almost seven times. In the highest leadership level in the country it increased by a factor of twelve. Particularly since the year 2000, when Putin was elected to the presidency, the transfer of military officers to the economy and politics has occurred "on a massive scale". The penetration of former military and security service officers into government and business has now gone so far that Kryshtanovskaya has suggested the term "militocracy" (rule by the military) for the Putin regime.[12] With so many officers in positions of power, it is no surprise that loyalty has become a guiding principle of the state.

Elena Chinyaeva, a Russian economist, has identified the main problem of the country as the absence of an official economic policy. If there is such a policy at all, it consists of a single principle, namely that of non-interference with natural market forces – provided the economic actors are loyal to the President. The President has a very vocal and provocative economic advisor, Andrey Illarionov, but "between the radical views of Illarionov and the no-action policy of the Russian government, the Russian economy continues to wander in the dark without clear guidance." Chinyaeva speaks of a "paradoxical symbiosis," a "synergy of inaction" where the liberalism of Illarionov converges with "the notorious concept of Russian fatalism."[13]

Indeed, there is no economic policy except one of *laissez-faire* in an environment where the authoritarian President demands first and foremost loyalty from economic actors. The regulatory environment of economic activity may be improving under Putin. But even if it were ideal within a few years, potential investors hit the barrier of the country's hard geographic facts. It is very unlikely that, with the free movement of capital world-wide, the Russian state will be able to offer the massive concessions that will be needed to induce the large capital inflows that would be required to build up an infrastructure. Russia's political actors will continue to deal with the country's economic and social problems in an ineffective way. Its population will have to show even more patience and endurance.

---

[12] Kryshtanovskaya, Ol'ga, 'Rezhim Putina, liberal'naya militokratiya?' in: *Pro et Contra* Vol. 7, No. 4, Autumn 2002, at http://pubs.carnegie.ru/p&c/ (retrieved 26.06.2003).
[13] Chinyaeva, Elena, *o.c.*

RUSSIA IN THE TRANSFORMING INTERNATIONAL SECURITY SYSTEM

The Role of Russia in the Present International Security System.

Irina Kobrinskaya

The situation of Russia in the transforming international security system is in a sense unique: Russia has started its transformation, but it is finding its place in a new system under construction with great difficulty.

The current transformation of the international security structure to a very significant extent was caused and preconditioned by the dissolution of the Soviet Union and the so called "socialist camp" and its security and economic structures – the Warsaw Treaty Organisation and Comecon. Before 1991 the Soviet Union and the United States had formed the focal point of the bipolar security system for 50 years. With the dissolution of the Soviet Union, the basis for the former security structure was annihilated. Nevertheless, it still exists and its institutions, first and foremost NATO, function. This fact gave grounds to the arguments of those in Russia who severely criticised and stubbornly opposed the process of NATO enlargement, particularly in the latter quarter of the 1990s, when NATO enlargement was the key issue in Russian-Western relations.

We may conclude that, due to the dispute over NATO enlargement as well as the illusions about the "end of history" at the beginning of the decade, the 1990s were mostly wasted time for the transformation of the international security system in order to adapt it to new challenges, risks and threats, which in their turn have been rapidly changing.

In the first half of the 1990s the main threats, caused predominantly by the processes in the former socialist countries, were the following. Firstly, the socio-economic and political instability, particularly in the New Independent States (NIS) and in South-Eastern Europe and the threat of an uncontrolled migration flow to the West, constituting "soft and non-traditional threats" such as illegal drugs and arms trafficking, the risk of diseases, ecological threats, etc.. Secondly, ethnic-national tensions (e.g. in the Carpathian region, in the Northern Caucasus, Central Asia) and conflicts between and within the weak NIS, where new quasi-state formations (Nagorno-Karabakh, Transdnestria, Abkhazia) have struggled for independence (from correspondingly Azerbaijan, Moldova and Georgia). The prime example of the large-scale conflict, caused by the state dissolution process in the 1990s was the war in former Yugoslavia. Another example, at least in its first stage, was the war in Chechnya. This phenomenon and threat has been given the definition "failed states".

At the same time, the difficulties of meeting those risks and threats signalled to the international security community the need to start transformation. In spite of its resistance to NATO enlargement, Russia started an uneven rapprochement with the alliance. As early as May 1997 Russia and NATO signed the Founding Act in Paris and the Permanent Joint Council was established. Although it did not stimulate practical cooperation, this first step played a significant symbolic role and served as an additional contact channel. NATO, for its part, started to revise its concept. Its goals and mission have been transformed *de facto*, and later *de jure*, from defence of the member states to peace-making – conflict regulation and crisis management, particularly beyond the NATO zone of responsibility. In 1999, after strong disagreements over Kosovo in the spring and the Russian raid on Pristina airport, both sides started to cooperate rather effectively in their peace-keeping mission. Nevertheless, Russia strongly opposed the internationalisation of the peace-making activities in the post-Soviet area.

Towards the end of the 1990s - the beginning of 21st century stabilisation in Eastern Europe - the accelerating globalisation process together with the positioning of the United States as a unique superpower, raised concerns regarding threats, rooted in anti-globalist, anti-American and in general anti-Western civilisation moods within different groups, mostly linked to the Islamic world.

In this new situation and faced with new threats, Russia, in spite of a deepening gap between Russia and the West in the period 1998 (after financial crisis) – 2001 (until September 11), objectively emerged on the Western side of the global divide.

Still, on the part of the West, the question remains whether or not the new Russia will replace the former Soviet Union – trying to restore its influence in the post-Soviet area and to project its power further to the East, South and West, to Central Eastern Europe. These concerns hamper the transformation of the international security system. But they are understandable. Partly they are based on phantom fears and lack of trust; partly on the fact that, in spite of drastic a reduction of its population (practically by half – from roughly 270 to less than 147 million), territory, GDP and armed forces,[1] Russia did not cease to be the traditional structure-forming element of the international security system, due to the following considerations:
- the Russian nuclear potential;
- conventional weapons and forces;
- Russia's participation in the treaties maintaining the arms control system, in spite of its growing imperfection and inadequacy: although the ABM is dead, there is still Strategic Nuclear Potential, the Conventional Forces in Europe, the Nuclear Non-Proliferation Treaties;

---

[1] Reportedly, staff numbers in the armed forces were cut practically by three (from 2.8 million in 1992 to 1.162 million in 2002), but according to the London International Institute of Strategic Studies, the real or list numbers of Russian armed forces are even lower than staff figures.

- Russia's membership of key institutions of international security – UN Security Council, OSCE, G8, Russia – NATO Council, as well as its membership of regional organisations in the field of foreign policy and security – the CIS, Russian-Belorussian Union, Organisation of Collective Security Treaty, Shanghai Treaty Organisation; Russia actively participates in Asian Pacific and Northern European–Baltic forums;
- Russia proved to be needed in the new type of structures, the *ad hoc* coalitions formed and dealing with burning critical issues, such as operation in Afghanistan. The United States tried hard to make Russia an ally or supporter in their operation in Iraq;
- Russia remaining the international security tendencies generator, particularly in Europe and Central Asia. It is a centre, attracting and pulling for various reasons, including security (conflict resolution, crisis-regulation, external border problems, organised crime, illegal migration, drugs and arms trafficking and other traditional and non-traditional, hard and soft security threats and risks), some states (Belorussia, Moldova, Armenia, Kazakhstan, Kyrgyzstan, Tajikistan and even Georgia settling problems with Abkhazia) and – until recently[2] – pushing away the others (in Central Europe, the Baltic states). This magnetism and, vice versa, anti-magnetism influences the dynamics of security processes, accelerates them (as in the case of NATO enlargement and accession of the CEE and Baltic states to the EU) or, on the contrary, slows them down, whether this is positive or negative. Ukraine, for example, is in a position where it is under both the centripetal and centrifugal impact of Russia. This, to a significant extent, preconditions its ambivalent policy towards NATO, the US and even the EU. Thus, Russia intentionally or non-intentionally influences the dynamics of international security transformation.

Since Russia, on the one hand, tries to keep its system-forming position and significance but, on the other hand, aims to define its new role, it needs the system. Naturally, it attempts to keep the old system of security institutions and mechanisms – the United Nations, the arms control treaties and, in this way, Russia objectively slows down the transformation of the international security system. Russian politicians and experts, taking into account the experience of the last decade and current developments, believe that, in the event of drastic transformation, the place of the old traditional security system will be taken by no-one. This, because the United States cannot substitute or replace the system - at least, it cannot be a stable and long-term substitute. According to some Russian analysts, in the foreseeable future the transforming international security system will live through the changing periods of the US

[2] After NATO accession and the decision on their EU membership the Central European and Baltic states, assured of their "belonging" in Europe, are redefining their posture towards Russia to a more pragmatic and unbiased one. Moreover, many of them, in their positioning in the EU, regard Russia now as an 'asset', rather than as a threat. See: 'Russia and Central Eastern Europe', Briefing of the Foundation for Prospective Studies and Initiatives, 2002; 'Russia and the Baltic: 2010', Report of the Foundation for Prospective Studies and Initiatives, 2003, www.psifoundation.ru.

unipolar leadership and find a balance between the US and other centres of power. Firstly, because the United States is not likely to take up leadership in all cases when international security is threatened and, secondly, because they will need cooperation with and support from other great powers.[3]

This is the reason – if we try to put into logical terms the opposition of ideologically biased left and right nationalist political forces in Russia – why Russia resists the unipolar security system: it does not leave Russia an independent system-forming role.

Although the general feeling is the need for a security system, mostly understood in traditional, i.e. 20th century terms, Russia definitely differs from Central European former socialist countries in the sense that there is no con-sensus on foreign and security policy. The Central European states, in spite of all contradictions and crises, are highly united in terms of their foreign and security policy priorities, these being membership of NATO and of the European Union. In the words of the well-known Polish publicist and member of 'Solidarnost', Zdislaw Naider, referring to Poland, the European Union or NATO membership is not a diagnosis for Russia. Better, or most likely worse, Russia can survive without being a part of these institutions. At the same time, for Ukraine, the diagnosis is both EU and Russia, which stresses its foreign policy dichotomy.

Nevertheless, an important change in Russia as compared to the 1990s is that its participation in international institutions is not regarded in terms of "Eurasianism" or "Westernism" but rather in terms of "individualism" (or, to go even further, "unilateralism") or "institutionalism". This new paradigm in security and foreign policy discourse depends mostly on self-estimation, on the strength or weakness of Russia. Analysis of the Russian debate on security and foreign policy shows that a strong, powerful Russia, i.e. the assessment which depends on the individual perception of the country by analysts or politicians, can afford an independent course, while a weak Russia has to place itself within the international institutions.

This marks a paradox, an obvious contradiction to the thesis that Russia needs the international security system to define its new role and policy.

Does that mean that President Eltsin – or, even more so – President Putin, struggling for cooperation with the West, for a place in G8, are in Lenin's terminology *"porazhentsy" or "losers"*? Are they those who admit Russia's weakness? Or is there another logic to their policy?

Apart from the institutional-individual approach, the need for Russia in the international security system and institutions and its place therein is also estimated and perceived in the paradigm of threat evaluation.

---

[3] Pushkov, A., 'Does America need the Spectre of World Hegemony?' in: *Nezavisimaya Gazeta*, June 19, 2003.

The traditional conservative approach of the military in Russia presupposes that the threat comes from the West, the USA and Europe, although the motivation has changed. This is not based on Cold War paradigms, but rather on the geopolitical concepts of the beginning of the 20th century (from MacKinder to Russian philosophers).

Such an approach presupposes the structure and tasks of the Armed Forces, viewed similarly to the previous bipolar deterrence period, which means maintaining a large army of over one million, able to deter threats in three main theatres – Western Europe, the Pacific (US, Japan) and China. Simultaneously, the proponents of this approach accept that both now and in the mid-term future the southern flank remains the most dangerous for Russian security.

This security posture obviously relies predominantly on Russian military potential and its abilities, supported possibly by Belorussia and Armenia. Nevertheless, it is hardly shared by the other members of the Organisation of Collective Security Treaty in Central Asia, who host the US and NATO countries' forces on their territories, as well as bases involved in the stabilisation operation in Afghanistan.

Thus, such a security policy scenario leaves Russia without strong and reliable partners in the West.

The modern approach, articulated by President V. Putin and shared by the majority of the political elite, considers that the threats to Russian security come predominantly from the South. In general, most are actually non-traditional threats. At present and in the foreseeable future, Russia will scarcely be involved in large-scale conflicts; low-intensity conflicts are most likely. Simultaneously, international terrorism is regarded as the most dangerous threat.

This point of view defines a different set of requirements for the Armed Forces and international security policy. It accentuates the need for modernisation of the Armed Forces, for high-precision arms and electronic surveillance systems, effectively coordinated with the systems of fire guidance and for raising professional standards in the Armed Forces. At the same time, the proponents of this approach on the right political flank estimate that Russia will not need an army of more than 550-600 thousand. The reduction of the Army and its transfer from conscription to contract form the core of the concept of military reform, strongly supported by the reformist political forces in Russia. Not surprisingly, the military opposes these plans. The military reform, started as early as the second half of the 1980s, during Gorbachev's perestroika, has mostly failed. Deterioration of the Armed Forces became commonplace and a characteristic of the situation in the Russian military sphere. Numerous re-structurings or rather "reshuffles" did not solve but rather aggravated the problems. In fact, this matter has been the focal point of public debates for the past two years and it is likely to become one of the key issues of the election campaign for the State Duma in December 2003.

74

This approach presupposes partnership and cooperation in the security field between Russia and the West in fighting common threats, first and foremost terrorism.

The lack of consensus on security policy in Russia, along with the lack of trust, strengthens the doubts on the part of the West regarding cooperation with Moscow, in spite of its consequential official rhetoric and policy. Even in the Iraqi case, Kremlin opposition to military operations was no stronger than that of Paris or Berlin. Moreover, at the end of May 2003, during the 300th anniversary summit meetings in St. Petersburg, Russia managed to lessen the tension between US, German and French leaders, which positively influenced the climate of the G8 summit in France.

The question of whether the policy of the Kremlin will not change for reasons other than a lack of public support is an important factor for Russian partners in the world. What could these reasons be? A second factor is the moods within society; after all Putin's era will end and, as democratic societies, as countries formulating their policies on the basis of democratic values, the Western states are not indifferent to this aspect.

To better understand the logic and nature of Russian security and foreign policy and to estimate its stability, it is necessary to answer the following questions: How is security and foreign policy perceived by public opinion? Is Russian official security policy reliable and can it be trusted by the West as consistent and long-term? How does this policy correspond to the transformation of the international security system? What can be done both by Russia and the West to transform the international security system so that it corresponds to the new security demands? Finally, is there a special role for cooperation between the EU and Russia in this field?

Correlation between Russian Foreign and Security Policy and Domestic Policy

The dependence of Russian foreign policy-making on domestic policy or, in particular, on the forthcoming parliamentary and presidential elections, which was rather significant in the 1990s, has substantially diminished due to several factors.

Firstly, objectively, the tragic events of September 11, 2001 provided the amorphous decaying system of international relations with a missing traditional element – a common enemy, i.e. terrorism. Russia unquestionably fell into the camp of the vulnerable. The nature of the threat, in contrast to the former Yugoslavian conflicts of the 1990s, potentially and actually does not divide but, rather, unites Russia with the West. Although still in need of coherent definition or possibly, on the contrary, due to the vague multi-location and unexpected character of the threat, terrorism serves as a consolidating element not only for the civilised international community, but also for national entities. In fact, the American tragedy, not to mention the October 2002 Nord-Ost tragedy in Moscow, have shown the direction for the solution to the most painful Russian problem, Chechnya. Defined as a manifestation of the global security threat, of international terrorism, the Chechen war has been to a significant extent conceived as a major domestic problem, i.e. as a problem of the political regime. Simultaneously, Chechnya lost its validity as a controversial issue on duty in Russian-Western relations. First the United States then Europe have downgraded the Chechen problem to an argument about the non-democratic nature of Russian power. This does not justify the crimes on both federal and Chechen sides of the conflict, but diversifies the methods for their settlement. Moreover, in this paradoxical way, the Chechen conflict has been finally internationalised; it has become a matter of international security. Consequently, the chances of its settlement are likely to increase.

Secondly, in 2000-2001, Putin's Administration intentionally lowered the profile of foreign policy. On the one hand, this was caused by a crisis in Russian-Western relations: "Russian fatigue", particularly after the 1998 financial crisis, and strong reservations in the West regarding the new Russian President, especially his professional special services past, is a concern, as articulated in a famous question, "Who is Mr. Putin?" In addition, the new Russian leadership was well aware of the ineffectiveness of further anti-NATO-enlargement stakes, either as a policy course or as a domestic public relations matter, i.e. the generally unattractive state of the foreign policy sphere for public relations in Russia. On the other hand, the economic boom of 2000-2001, after the crisis, served as a sufficient graphic argument for the effectiveness of the new Administration. Finally, the Kremlin used the pause in its relations with the West to concentrate on inter-regional relations, to build the so-called "power vertical", partly lessening, due to weakened dialogue with the West, the severe criticism and blame heaped upon autocratic policies for their part.

Thirdly, the Kremlin sticks consistently to a positive integrative and cooperative foreign policy line and rhetoric which, mostly due to the objective situation, turned out to be rather effective. In addition, the same situation deprived the opposition of any coherent alternative. The same concerns the mass media. What is illustrative here is the coincidence in the data from public opinion polls: when asked on 28 April 2003 what was the attitude towards US operations in Iraq of a) President Putin, b) the majority of Russian officials and c) the Russian mass media, the respondents estimated them respectively as "supportive", 2%, 2%, 2%; "reserved", 39%, 30%, 25%, and "negative" 53%, 56%, 63%. This similarity can be interpreted as a loyalty and obedience from the elite and mass media to the Kremlin or, on the contrary, as the populism of power. Nevertheless, the official line has not significantly deviated over the course of a year. The position of the radical left, supporting Saddam Hussein, was not taken into consideration. Finally, earlier the Kremlin took a much more radical decision, supporting the US operation in Afghanistan and agreeing, notwithstanding severe criticism from the left and from the military, to the allocation of US bases in Central Asia.

Fourthly, political stabilisation and the new socio-economic transition period was a precondition for the decline in the public activity level (which becomes a domestic policy problem, particularly in the election period) and indifference to policy, including foreign policy matters. Russian society, as well as the West, is past the illusion and disillusion periods and has entered a more sober and realistic stage in its expectations regarding the West. Public opinion polls demonstrate sharp falls in attitudes towards the US, similar to those of the Kosovo crisis period or those caused by the scandals during the Olympic Games of 2002. The same happened during the Iraqi war. But these declines are short-lived. In fact, it is difficult to distinguish Russian public opinion reaction from that of traditional Western democracies. The Pew Research Regions public opinion polls demonstrate very close similarity in the approach towards the US in Russia, Germany and France for the period summer 2002 – June 2003. The lowest point for opinions of the US, in March 2003, coincided in time – and the Russian public demonstrated negativism (only 28% positive) – with France (31%) and Germany (25%). At the same time, when asked how Russian-American relations would develop after the beginning of the Iraqi war, only 29% answered that the tension would grow, while 53% said that they would again normalise. Russian public opinion has become much more reserved regarding Russia's involvement in the crises and conflicts. Only 1-2% supported Russian involvement in the operation, between 33% and 42% (at its lowest in March 2003) supported the option "to stay outside, but remain a US ally in the anti-terrorist coalition", and 2-6% chose the answer to support Iraq by arms transfers, etc.

Fifthly, the stable high rating of President Putin adds to his constitutional authority in the foreign policy and security sphere. In three and a half years, Putin's ratings have not dropped below 60% and the average is over 70%. He remains the most trusted Russian politician (on average 50% of the respondents trust Putin), this indicator is practically 3 times higher than that for the next ranked name. Although less than 50% (48%) say that Putin fulfilled their expectations, his April 2003 rating was 75%. It is noteworthy that foreign policy is regarded as a single unquestionably successful sphere of his activities.

Thus, as a result of these factors, but predominantly the last mentioned here, the Kremlin's dependence on domestic policy, which was so high in the 1990s (say in 1995 or 1999, in connection with the Kosovo crisis), is much smaller. Although the Kremlin can afford unpopular foreign and security policy steps (e.g. the decision to withdraw Russian bases from Cuba and Vietnam were strongly criticised in political and military circles), in general its foreign policy is supported by public opinion. Also, in spite of the lack of consensus on foreign policy within the political elite, opposition to the Kremlin is rather moderate and has no coherent alternative strategy. All this serves as a guarantee for consistent and stable Russian foreign and security policy.

The logic of Russian Security and Foreign Policy

The logic of Russian security and foreign policy is even more important for the West. It has profoundly changed compared to the 1990s. The foreign and security policy practice of 2000-2003 demonstrates that pragmatism has taken over the remnants of the superpower ambitions, while economy has become the main priority of foreign policy. The tendency towards the economisation of foreign and security policy is proving stable and long-lasting. Putin's policy is based on the assumption that it is not so much the military force, but rather the economy which defines the real weight of a state in international relations. Thus, Russia has only a slight chance of maintaining its present position or strengthening it without economic modernisation, i.e. building a post-industrial age economy. This cannot be achieved without Russia's integration into the global economy.

In practice, this means stable, sustainable relations with the EU, membership of the WTO, a solution to the Kaliningrad problem, the creation of favourable conditions for Russian business abroad and for foreign business and investments in Russia; in other words, Russia's introduction into the system of Western institutions. Russian domestic reforms (tax, legal, etc.) demonstrate a movement in this direction.

Moreover, the constant topic of Russian-Western relations, WTO membership and the building of a common economic space with the EU, can be interpreted as an attempt to create an additional stimulus and, simultaneously, an instrument of enforcement for domestic reforms to adapt the Russian economy to Western standards, norms and rules.

Functionally, foreign and security policy is defined as an instrument for creating favourable conditions for successful domestic development and for improving the living conditions of the Russian people. This logic corresponds to the interests of Russian business, which actively participates in foreign and security policy debates.

At the same time, some very important factors cause profound confusion regarding Russian foreign and security policy. Firstly, the official documents obviously lag behind and contradict practice. Thus, already at the beginning of his presidential term, Putin made a number of far-reaching declarations, among them concerning eventual Russian membership of NATO. Analysts in the West regarded these declarations as not coincidental, aimed at establishing friendly personal contacts with Western leaders and articulating the main message – that Russia intends to cooperate with Western states and institutions.[4]

At the same time, the National Security Concept, adopted and approved by Presidential Decree no. 24 on 10 January 2000, mentions among the main

---

[4] See e.g.: MacFarlane, S. Neil, 'Beyond Enlargement: NATO's Role in Russia's Relations with the West', Geneva Centre for Security Policy, Occasional Paper Series, no. 24, August 2000, p. 6.

threats the "strengthening of military-political blocks and alliances, first and foremost NATO expansion to the East." Meanwhile in the Military Doctrine, adopted on 21 April 2000, NATO is not mentioned. It is said that "presently the threat of traditional direct military aggression against Russia and its allies has diminished due to the positive changes in the international situation."

Most of the documents from Putin's presidency have a reactive and situation-linked nature. In the situations concerning the Kosovo and Chechen conflicts, the vocabulary of the Cold War re-emerged in the National Security Concept. But most comments in the West were generated by the consideration of the Russian Federation "of the possibility of using military force to provide its national security, … including nuclear weapons", the possibility of the "first use" of nuclear weapons.

The National Security Concept and Foreign Policy Concept, although adopted within 6 months, differ considerably. Experts consider that the most professional of all is the Military Doctrine (the so-called "Sergeev doctrine", after the ex-defence minister), which is nevertheless defined as transitional, taking into account financial and economic limitations.

The revision of the basic documents is becoming a vital necessity in order to avoid confusing misinterpretation abroad and, no less importantly, inside the country. At the same time, the rapid transformation of international security does not lend itself to the elaboration of fundamental documents. Thus, the increasing stake on military power on the part of the United States contradicts the dominant tendencies of the 1990s.

A second factor causing confusion regarding Russian foreign and security policy is the remaining non-transparent Byzantine style of the decision-making process. A lack of coordination, high-quality expertise, initiative and delegation of responsibility for decisions to a higher level – all these problems have been aggravated during Putin's presidency and can be explained partly as negative consequences of the concentration of power in the Kremlin. They are estimated by Russian experts as the most serious drawbacks of Russian foreign and security policy-making.[5]

The previous period, current practice and the experience with several crises in international relations during the period 2000-2003, as well as prognoses regarding a second term by President Putin, give no grounds for forecasting major changes in Russian foreign and security policy.

---

[5] 'Russia in 2003 and Its Foreign Policy', Survey published in: *Russia in Global Affairs*, no. 1, December 2002; excerpts from the Report by the Foundation for Prospective Studies and Initiatives. Full text in Russian available on www.psifoundation.ru

Does Russian Foreign and Security Policy Correspond to the Transformation of the International Security System?

The rapidly changing international situation leaves Russia with its focus on the economy and the rest of the world, predominantly Europe, behind the US with its obvious stake on military power, readiness to use force and unilateralism in decision-making. It is obvious that, in the foreseeable future, neither Russia nor Europe will be able (and hardly intends) to bridge the growing gap in military capabilities. In its turn, the increasing misbalance in military spending and power aggravates the tensions between the Western allies within NATO. The enlargement of the Northern Alliance has added to the political controversies, as vividly demonstrated during the Iraqi war. Although criticizing the United States, traditional European democracies ("the old Europe") are dependent and reliant on the US in the security field.

In fact, analysts have forecast such problems before September 11, 2001. "In sum we have arrived at a system of democracies without having a democratic system of international relations."[6] "The Cold War bargain struck between a recovering Europe and a hegemonic America is fast wearing thin... If the Atlantic link is to be maintained, the US and Europe must be prepared to strike a new and more equitable deal. Leaders on both sides of the Atlantic must face this reality..."[7] The American position regarding European Security and Defence Policy has been changing from moderately positive to rather negative and the analysts did not rule out the possibility that the US would "most probably be in the position to block or constrain it with the assistance of some pro-Atlanticist members of the EU." Meanwhile, the main concerns in Europe are the illusion that European "defence capability may result in the situation in which higher intensity cases will not be adequately addressed by anybody."[8] Already in 2000, it was stressed that if the Russian Federation, as a major external player, "gives the impression that Europe without the US is a better place, the determination of the EU member countries to carry European defence into effect may quickly vanish."[9]

All this poses difficult questions for Russia. Seemingly, following the traditional logic of Russian foreign and security policy, the perspective of a weakened Northern Atlantic alliance, trans-Atlantic contradictions could suit Moscow. Nevertheless, the new logic of Russian security and foreign policy and practice shows that this assumption is not true. At present and in the foreseeable future Russia will not gain from a trans-Atlantic split, it would be counter to Russian national security interests. The Iraqi crisis proved this thesis.

---

[6] Dunay, Pal, 'U.S.-EU Relations after the Introduction of the Euro and Reinvention of European Security and Defence', Geneva Centre for Security Policy, Occasional Paper Series, No.23, August 2000, p. 9.

[7] Kupchan, Chrales A., 'In Defense of European Defense: An American Perspective' in: *Survival*, vol. 42, no. 2, Summer 2000, pp. 17-18.

[8] Dunay, Pal, *o.c.*, p. 10.

[9] *Ibid.*

In the dynamically transforming international security system, in the foreseeable future the United States remains the absolute leader:

- Although provoking anti-Western and anti-globalist sentiments, the US has demonstrated its willingness and ability to form and lead *ad hoc* coalitions against terrorist groups;
- Only through partnership and cooperation with the US can Russia resist the threat of the proliferation of weapons of mass destruction (WMD);
- Without the active participation of the United States it is impossible to build a new international security system with institutions able to meet new challenges and threats or to modernise the existing institutions, first and foremost the UN and NATO. Many Russian experts express a very sceptical attitude towards the UN, OSCE or NATO and envisage no system *per se* in the future, stressing that the system of the second half of the 20th century was rather an exception to the rule. At the same time, the dominant majority thinks it is necessary to develop new principles and structures for international security. Preserve the best – trust building measures, incentives for disarmament, security of nuclear arsenals;
- Without cooperation with the United States, it is impossible to integrate China into a global security system, which remains a huge challenge for Russia and for the rest of the world.

NATO is presently regarded in Russia as the only capable international military institution. In spite of plans to re-allocate bases from Germany to Poland, closer to Russian borders, which three or four years ago would have provoked a very negative reaction in Moscow, Russia actively cooperates with the Alliance within the new Russia-NATO Council which, unlike the Permanent Joint Council of 1997, is perceived as a prospective pro-institution of Russia-West security cooperation.

At the same time, it is widely accepted and reiterated in official declarations and documents that Europe (the European Union) remains the key priority for Russian foreign policy. Apart from the fact that Europe is Russia's biggest economic and trade partner, they have many common security problems in the Middle East, the Caucasus and Central Asia. Russia and Europe still face the shared threat of international terrorism, the perception of which in Russia is closer to that of Europeans than of Americans; to a large extent it is preconditioned by the problems of large Islamic entities/minorities. Russia is also interested in cooperation with Europe in conflict prevention and resolution and in peace-keeping. Of special importance for Russia are the plans for European missile defence.

In the transforming international security system, the best policy for Russia is not to divide, not to make a choice, but to maintain international security integrity and to build into it. There is no evidence or arguments that Russia plans to deviate from this route.

MAKING A GOOD ENTRANCE. RUSSIA'S RE-ENGAGEMENT WITH THE WORLD ECONOMY AND, UNFORTUNATELY, WITH EUROPE IN PARTICULAR[1]

Philip Hanson

Russia is not, at the time of writing, a member of the right clubs. It is not in the World Trade Organisation (WTO), it is not in the European Union, not in the OECD, not in NATO and only half in the G7½. For a country that is re-entering society after 70 years of semi-isolation, and that is economically small (0.8% of world output at the exchange rate, 2.6% of world output at purchasing power parity in 2000, according to the World Bank), this is an economic handicap.

It is probably more of a handicap than it would have been in an earlier age. Individuals may have taken to Bowling Alone, but countries have become more clubbable. From 1868, when the Meiji Restoration ended Japan's centuries-old seclusion, the Japanese were able to turn their country into a successful, late-industrialising, catching-up nation without having to submit to a set of rules devised by a club of wealthy states. They put up trade barriers, kept out foreign direct investment, bought in foreign science and technology and started new industries with state investment. Even their successors as late industrialisers a century or so later, such as Korea, Taiwan and Singapore, also largely set their own economic rules.

In contrast, Russia is at present growing, opening up and changing economically, but its policymakers believe – with good reason – that it is essential to seek membership of the WTO and a closer relationship with the EU; in both cases Russia is being asked to re-arrange its affairs to meet rules set by others. For WTO accession it is being asked to raise domestic energy prices, cut tariffs, restrict farm subsidies far below US or EU rates and open its more attractive sectors more fully to foreign business. To develop a Common European Economic Space with the EU, it is being asked (as things stand at present) to adopt a great deal of the EU's commercial and social legislation – the *acquis communautaire* – and is not being offered free trade in return.

Russia's situation as an outsider looking in has clear economic disadvantages. Outside the WTO, it cannot make use of the organisation's machinery for resolving trade disputes. Dealing at arm's length with the EU, it confronts EU protectionism, restricting its sales of farm products, chemicals and steel to the largest nearby market.

---

[1] This chapter also appears, in a slightly different form, in Motyl, Alex, Blair Ruble and Lilia Shevtsova (eds.), *Transformation and Integration. Russia and the West after 9/11*.

The more successful ex-communist countries of Central Europe and the Baltic region have joined the OECD, the WTO and the EU. The process by which they qualified for EU membership brings out clearly the analogy with an individual joining a club, right down to the ritual humiliation inflicted on would-be members of fraternity houses: in this case, being beaten over the head, for several years, with 31 chapters of the *acquis*. A milder version of this hazing seems to be the best Brussels can offer Russia, as a condition of becoming merely a slightly closer outsider.

This preamble may suggest that I want to present Russia as a victim. That is not the case. Nations, like individuals, may be kept out of the best clubs for good reason. The desirability of WTO membership and of a Common European Economic Space for Russia is clear, and Russia's readiness to benefit from these associations remains to be judged. The aim of this paper is to review Russia's changing economic links with the outside world and to consider ways in which policymakers inside and outside Russia might act to alter those links so as to promote Russia's development as a capitalist, market economy.

The paper is organised as follows. The first section is a brief assessment of the state of play in Russia's domestic economic transformation in early 2003. The second section is a review of the level and composition of Russian transactions with other countries: trade, investment and the movement of people. Links with Europe are stressed because they predominate. For powerful reasons of economic geography, Russia is stuck with the countries to its west in the European land-mass as (collectively) its main economic partner. The third section summarises the main economic issues in Russian-European relations, with some comments also on Russia and the US. The final section is a summary of conclusions about prospects and policy choices.

The Russian Economy since 1998

I have assessed the recent performance and medium-term prospects of the Russian economy at length elsewhere.[2] This section is a summary of the main points in that assessment that are relevant to Russia's international economic integration.

The financial crisis of August 1998 was a punishment for poor Russian economic policy-making. From mid-1995 onwards, the rouble had been "stabilised" within a slowly-descending exchange-rate corridor; the authorities had stopped financing budgetary deficits by printing money; they had not, however, stopped running deficits; these were financed chiefly by three- or six-month securities known as GKOs; foreign investors were allowed into the rouble-denominated GKO market and, for a time, made very high returns in it; much of the manufacturing industry was saved from closure by being allowed

---

[2] Hanson, Philip, 'The Russian Economic Recovery: Do Four Years' Growth Tell us that the Fundamentals have Changed?' in: *Europe-Asia Studies*, Vol. 55 Issue 3, May 2003, pp. 365-82.

to underpay taxes and energy costs; the government deficits were directly and indirectly a reflection of these tacit subsidies; in effect, the natural-resource sector was used to prop up a large population of manufacturing enterprises that were thereby spared the sink-or-swim pressures of real market competition.

In August 1998, that curious collective animal, the market, decided that neither the rouble exchange rate against the dollar nor the redemption of the mounting pyramid of GKOs was sustainable. The exchange rate was allowed to fall and quickly went from six roubles to the dollar to about 25. At the time of writing it is at about 31. Russia defaulted on part of its sovereign debt.

After the crisis, Russia experienced its first officially-recorded output growth since 1989 (apart from a brief, marginal upturn in 1997). In 1999-2002, inclusive-GDP growth averaged just under 6% a year. The trigger for the recovery was the huge devaluation of the rouble. This made imports suddenly much more expensive. That in turn offered Russian processing industry – engineering, food-processing, clothing and the like – an opportunity to come back from the dead and use their large, under-utilised capacity for the production of import-substitutes. This, to the surprise of many, they managed to do. A mass of previously moribund enterprises, hitherto kept alive by large and systematic non-payment, over-valued barter settlements and other ingenious and government-tolerated deviations from standard market behaviour, began to generate cash again. In this way, a policy failure, resulting in a forced devaluation, kick-started recovery.

In 1999, an upturn in oil prices provided further assistance. Therefore the recovery was led by net exports (exports less imports). This led many analysts to argue that the unexpected Russian growth spurt would fade away when either oil prices fell again for a prolonged period or the real appreciation of the rouble against the dollar and the euro (rouble depreciation insufficient to offset the higher rate of inflation in Russia, or even nominal rouble appreciation while Russian inflation stayed comparatively high) eroded the boost to Russian competitiveness provided by the devaluation.[3]

In 2001 and 2002, however, Russia survived some dips, admittedly brief, in oil prices, and net exports declined as the rouble appreciated in real terms, but domestic demand (household consumption, government spending and investment) continued to drive the economy. The growth of investment – by as much as 17% year on year in 2000 – was a particularly striking change from the past.[4] Capital flight, meanwhile, fell in 2001-02. The importance of Cyprus as a

---

[3] In principle, changes in oil prices and in the real exchange rate could neatly offset one another. This has not however happened in practice. See: Rautava, Jouko, 'The Role of Oil Prices and the Real Exchange Rate in Russia's Economy', Bank of Finland, BOFIT Discussion Paper no. 3, 2002.

[4] The growth of fixed investment slowed markedly in 2002 – officially to 2.5%. There are reasons however to doubt the reliability of this figure. See: Hanson, Philip, o.c., 2003. In January-February 2003 it was 9.5 % up, year on year. See: Economic Expert Group, www.eeg.ru, obzor 4 (retrieved 22.04. 2003).

source of inward foreign investment rose, indicating the return of some Russian-controlled offshore funds.

All of this occurred against a background of cautious macroeconomic policies and some acceleration of institutional reforms in Russia. The government has been running surpluses, paying down debt (in early 2003 foreign public debt was a modest 34% of GDP), moderating the growth of the money supply and limiting inflation: still in double digits (15.1% for consumer prices in 2002), but coming down. Gold and foreign exchange reserves rose sharply and are at levels almost sufficient to pay for a year's merchandise imports. Reforms of the tax system, of the land code, of business regulation (reducing the burden of registration, licensing, product certification and inspection) and of the judiciary have been pushed through a compliant Duma under an active president. Russians and foreigners doing business in Russia mostly report an improved business environment.

How sustainable is this progress? Sceptics maintain that there are major obstacles to Russia maintaining a trend rate of growth much above 3% a year in the long run, sufficient to keep the country on a catching-up trajectory.

The following are the main stylised facts that are usually cited in support of this view. The investment share of GDP (about 18%) remains modest; much infrastructure has decayed and needs large investment; the surge in import-substitute production has used up spare capacity in manufacturing but new investment there is lacking; the banks do little lending to the real sector, which might facilitate restructuring; large subsidies are still given to electricity and housing, distorting resource allocation; small-firm development has stagnated; above all, this remains a society in which informal rules prevail, allowing reforms to be legislated but not implemented, private interests to capture state agencies and property rights to remain blurred and insecure. Therefore, competitive market forces do not work effectively and this is not the kind of well-ordered society that can get out from under the natural-resource curse, as (for instance) Norway and the Netherlands have done.

The case for a more optimistic view rests, not on a denial that these are indeed the obstacles to Russian prosperity, but on evidence that changes are underway that are reducing their importance. In other words, it is a matter of assessing the nature and direction of change. The changes include the growth in investment and decline in capital flight referred to above. These suggest that the Russian business community is itself taking a more positive view. There are also signs of growth in small-firm employment in 2002; survey evidence that legislation to reduce the regulatory (and therefore the corruption) burden has really changed things on the ground;[5] the firm-level data indicating that leading Russian businessmen have, after much delay, tended to become real majority stake-holders in their firms, increasing their interest in the strengthening of property rights; the growth of bank lending to non-bank

---

[5] Six-monthly surveys by Cefir; see: www.cefir.ru

companies; the evidence of improved tax compliance by business. None of this evidence is yet conclusive, but the question whether the Russian economy really is, at last, modernizing, is open.

It is true that the lessons from world history are not encouraging. The institutional quality of national economies appears to be remarkably stable over time. Argentina does not (despite signs to the contrary in the 1990s) easily become Chile. But, for ex-communist countries, the relevance of the very long-term historical evidence is not clear. Most of them have already changed their economic institutions massively since the fall of communism. The great differences in their initial conditions around 1990 may go a long way to account for the wide variations amongst them in the rapidity of that change. It is possible that the long-delayed experience of domestic economic growth in Russia has had a benign effect: stimulating Russian businesspeople to take a longer-term view than before and, in effect, to have incentives to demand better economic institutions.

In as far as relations with the outside world are concerned, the changes for Russia have been massive. In the depths of Stalinism, in the late 1930s, links with the outside world were minimised; merchandise exports were as little as 0.5% of GNP.[6] After World War Two, trade expanded but chiefly with satellite countries. Intra-CMEA trade was extremely inefficient and the location of activity and geographical flows of transactions within the USSR were probably even more so. Part of post-communist change is the massive re-orientation of Russian trade flows that has already taken place (see the next section).

For much of the 1990s the IMF, the World Bank and to a lesser extent the European Bank for Reconstruction and Development worked on institutional change in the Russian economy by means of conditional aid – the success of which is much disputed. Now, market pressures operate more strongly. Large Russian companies increasingly have incentives to improve their financial reporting and their business practices in general. This applies whether they are hiring senior Western executives (as many are now doing), issuing American Depositary Receipts on Western equity markets, making direct share issues on foreign markets or issuing bonds or raising syndicated loans. Foreign portfolio and direct investment into Russia tends on the whole to exert similar pressures.

It is possible to argue, as some Russian critics do, that these growing market links operate to confine Russia to the role of "natural-resource appendage" to the established Western economies. One thesis in this paper is that Russia's exclusion so far from the WTO and its arm's-length relationship with the EU make it easier for Russian isolationists and proponents of a unique Russian way to argue with at least some plausibility along those lines. Conversely, reducing the barriers to Russian international economic integration weakens the Russian-way isolationists.

---

[6] Holzman, Franklyn D., 'Foreign Trade' in: Bergson A. and S. Kuznets (eds.), *Economic Trends in the Soviet Union*. Cambridge, Mass., Harvard University Press, 1963, p. 290.

The Present Economic Links between Russia and the West

Russians (more precisely, Russians mainly resident in Russia) have three main kinds of business and economic dealings with the West: trade in goods and services, cross-border investment (in both directions, both direct and port-folio) and travel for business, tourism and education. Within the trade category, transactions concerning fuel and energy are sufficiently important for each party to be looked at as a special subset.

Merchandise Trade

Foreign trade now looms large in the Russian economy. In 2002 merchandise exports plus imports were $152 billion and GDP at the exchange rate was $350 billion. The ratio of merchandise trade turnover to national income was therefore 43%. That measure is appropriate as an indicator of the importance of trade in generating income and absorbing expenditure and it shows Russia to be, by world standards, a rather small and rather open economy. If GDP were reckoned, however, not at the exchange rate but at purchasing power parity, the trade/GDP ratio would come down to well below 20%. This measure is more appropriate for indicating the external world's role in the allocation of Russian resources; it suggests a rather larger and only moderately-open economy.

The partner-composition of Russian trade has changed dramatically over the past decade. Trade with the other members of the CIS was just under 17% of the total last year – a remarkably low level when we consider that in early December 1991 these were all part of one country.

Table 1 gives a snapshot of the composition of Russian merchandise trade by trade-partner group in 2002. It will be seen that "Europe", in the sense of the present EU of 15 nations (EU15) plus Central and Eastern Europe (most of which will join the EU in 2004) and Norway and Switzerland, accounted for 54% of Russia's total merchandise trade, and two-thirds of its non-CIS merchandise trade. The gravitational pull of the US on the Russian economy, as far as merchandise trade is concerned, is small. The US economy may be somewhat larger than that of the EU15: $9.6 trillion against $8.5 trillion in 2000, according to the World Bank. But the US economy is much farther away. More precisely: it is much farther away than Europe from European Russia, where Russian population and income are concentrated.

It should be added that the data on Russian trade used here understate trade volumes. The Russian Central Bank calculates merchandise trade in 2002 at $107.2 billion for exports and $61.0 billion for imports – the latter including an estimate for "shuttle" (informal) trade.[7] Unfortunately, only the Customs data give a country breakdown.

---

[7] See: www.cbr.ru

Table 1. Russian merchandise trade in 2002, by trade-partner group ($ bn and %)[8]

Total trade ($ bn)	exports	105.8
	imports	46.0
	total turnover	151.8

Of which, with (% of turnover)

other CIS countries	16.9
Central-Eastern Europe	12.9
EU15	36.6
Norway + Switzerland	4.2
Asia-Pacific	16.4
US	4.6
other	8.4

Table 2. gives a snapshot – or rather, two snapshots, one from Moscow, one from Brussels – of Russia-EU trade in the year 2000.

Table 2. Russia-EU merchandise trade in the year 2000 ($ bn and %)[9]

			% change year on year	source
1.	Total Russian exports	103.0	41	Russian Customs
2.	o/w to EU15	36.9	48	"
3.	Total Russian imports	33.9	12	"
4.	o/w from EU15	11.1	-0.4	"
5.	Total EU exports	867.6		Eurostat
6.	o/w to Russia	18.2	34	"
7.	Total EU imports	945.5		"
8.	o/w from Russia	41.6	73	"
			% share	
Memorandum items				
RF exports to EU as % RF GDP			14 - 16	GDP & exchange rate from RECEP
RF imports from EU as % RF GDP			4 - 7	"

Notes: In the last two rows, the alternative figures for Russia-EU trade flows from previous rows are presented as proportions of the official rouble GDP converted at the average rouble-dollar exchange rate for the year (total Russian GDP = $260.7 bn).
The "mirror trade statistics" here give distorted reflections. In a tidy world, row 2 should equal row 8 and row 4 should equal row 6. Divergences of this order are not uncommon and do not necessarily indicate a peculiarly Russian data problem. Countries often differ in their methods of valuation, their recording of countries of destination and of origin and in the time at which a given flow is logged.

[8] *Source*: www.customs.ru (retrieved 23.04.2003)
[9] *Sources*: RECEP, *Russian Economic Trends. Monthly Update*, February 2002; UN ECE, *Economic Survey of Europe*, 2001, Issue 2, p. 31; http://europa.eu.int/comm/eurostat/datashop

88

The importance of Europe in the sense used above (EU15 + other East-Central Europe + Norway + Switzerland), not merely to Russian trade but to total Russian economic activity, is considerable. From the Russian customs data and dollar GDP at the exchange rate, exports to Europe were 15.4% of GDP in 2002 and imports 6.5%.

From Brussels' point of view, this trade is in aggregate rather small beer: 2-4% of total EU foreign trade and even smaller proportions of EU GDP – on a par with EU transactions with Norway.

One might therefore infer from these aggregate figures that if either party were the *demandeur* in the Russia-EU relationship, it would be Russia. I think this really is, on balance, the case. But the composition of the trade is such that this conclusion needs to be modified: the relationship is not so heavily one-sided as the total merchandise trade figures suggest.

Oil and Gas Trade

The reason for this is simple: the EU's heavy dependence on Russian energy, in the form of oil and gas. From figures on production, trade and usage given by Kari Liuhto for 1999, it can be deduced that Russia supplied about 11% of the oil used in the pre-enlargement EU of 15 countries and about 16% of gas consumption (NB: *not* imports but total usage).[10] Of course, the dependence is two-way: the seller needs the income, just as the buyer needs the product. Russia exports about a third of its gas production and almost two-thirds of its oil output. For both fuels, the dimensions of trade with Europe are substantial. Figures 1 and 2 illustrate this for the pre-enlargement EU15. The shares are higher (on both sides of the energy balance) for the enlarged EU.

Figure 1. The dimensions of Russia-EU oil flows in 1999[11]

Russian oil output: one-third to EU   **EU oil usage: 11% from Russia**

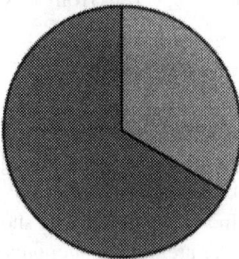

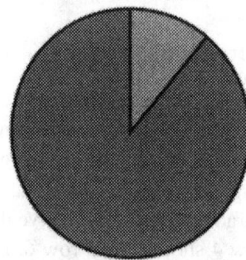

[10] Liuhto, Kari, 'Russian Oil and Gas – A Source of Integration', Research Report, Dept. of Industrial Engineering and Management, Lappeenranta University of Technology, 2002.
[11] *Source*: derived from Liuhto, Kari, *o.c.*

Figure 2. The dimensions of Russia-EU natural gas flows in 2001[12]

Russian gas output: 14% to EU **EU gas usage: 20% from Russia**

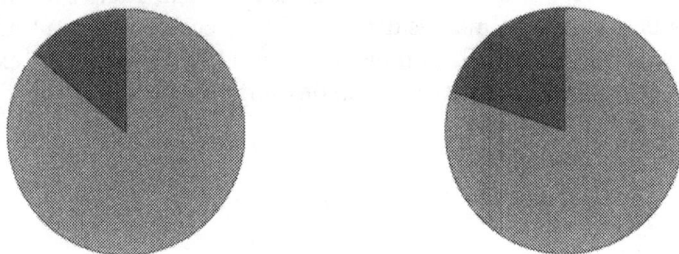

The locations of pipelines, oil terminals and gas reservoirs make it difficult for the supplier to switch markets in the short-to-medium term. To that extent, Russian dependence on Western European markets is strong in the medium term. In the longer run, it might be argued, Russia as a supplier may have more flexibility than Western Europe has as a customer. The other sources of supply to Western Europe offer little alternative in the longer term. As EU15 oil and gas consumption increases, Russia is the most likely source of additional supplies.[13] One study cites a projection of Russian gas exports to the EU (apparently the EU15) almost doubling by 2008, to about 200 bcm p.a..[14]

Does the US constitute an alternative energy market for Russia? It certainly does not in the foreseeable future, despite recent US Administration interest in exploring energy cooperation between the two countries. Transportation costs are higher to the US market, in part because of a remediable lack of large, deepwater oil terminals in Russia that would take large tankers. The present, experimental direct oil deliveries to the US by Yukos and LUKoil are based on transhipment from small to big tankers at sea. In January-July 2002 they amounted to only 0.7% of US oil imports and, of course, even less of total US oil consumption.[15]

The project to build a deepwater terminal at Murmansk and a pipeline to it, could in the medium term enable Russian oil companies to supply about 1 million b/d to US markets, at a transport cost below that from the Gulf to Houston.[16] That would still, however, only be about 5% of *current* US levels of

[12] *Source*: derived from BP (British Petroleum), *BP Statistical Review of World Energy, June 2002*. London, BP, 2002.
[13] Conversation with executives of a major energy company, April 2002.
[14] Samson, Ivan and Xavier Greffe, *Common Economic Space: Prospects of Russia-EU Relations. White Book*. Moscow, TACIS/RECEP, 2002, p. 11.
[15] Derived from *The Russia Journal*, October 10, 2002.
[16] Ariel Cohen, in a round-table on Russia and the Middle East at the Association for the Study of Nationalities Annual Convention, New York City, April 3-5, 2003.

oil consumption. With US usage and imports rising, it might in the medium term amount only to perhaps 5% of US oil imports.[17] Gravity rules, again.

The US matters much more to Russia for its influence in strategic developments in world oil and gas than for its foreseeable role as a trade partner in the usual sense. The US Administration and US oil majors, for example, have a considerable role in Caspian Basin developments, even where those do not involve direct Russia-US transactions.

Foreign investment

Russia has attracted relatively little foreign investment. Of the foreign investment that it has attracted, however, more than half has come from the present EU countries. Table 3 gives the cumulative totals of inward foreign investment to the end of September 2002.[18]

Table 3. Inward foreign investment into Russia, cumulative totals to end-Sept. 2002 ($ billion)[19]

	Foreign investment [a] of which	Foreign direct investment[b]
Total	39.80	19.39
of which, from		
Germany	6.84	1.58
Great Britain	4.81	2.10
France	3.39	0.27
Netherlands	2.81	2.42
Italy	1.51	0.19
Luxembourg	0.94	0.15
all identified EU countries	20.30	6.71
US	5.48	4.13

Notes: a. foreign direct investment + foreign portfolio investment + other (mostly loans).
b. foreign direct investment defined as the acquisition of a stake of 10% or more in a business.

---

[17] Telehami, Shibley, *et al.* (exchange of views), 'Does Saudi Arabia Still Matter?' in: *Foreign Affairs*, Vol. 81 Issue 6, Nov/Dec 2002, pp. 167-79.

[18] It should be added that Russian Central Bank statistics, www.cbr.ru, show a net inflow of capital into Russia in the second quarter of 2002 – a major change.

[19] *Source*: Goskomstat, *Sotsial'no-ekonomicheskoe polozhenie Rossii*, Jan-Sept. 2002.

There are numerous problems with definition and identification in foreign investment statistics. For what the Russian official numbers in Table 3 are worth, they indicate that the EU15 countries loom even larger in inward foreign investment into Russia than they do in Russian merchandise trade (see Tables 1 and 2).

The role of the US as a source of investment, particularly of direct investment, is more significant than it is as a trade partner. Indeed, the role of multinational companies with headquarters in the US may well be understated in Table 3. For example, the famous first McDonalds in Russia was opened by the Canadian McDonalds.

The destination of Russian outward capital flows is less well documented – not surprisingly, since part of those flows is illegal. It is safe to say, however, that the present EU is an important destination for Russian flight capital: not only in the form of houses in London and villas in the south of France, but also in the form of businesses, share portfolios and bank accounts. Such financial links with Western Europe may not matter to the great majority of Russians, but they matter to more than just a tiny elite. Russian scholars of my acquaintance seem without exception to have bank accounts in Western Europe.

Movement of People

It is a commonplace in Britain that just about every "public" (fee-paying) school has a Russian pupil or two. There is a scattering of Russian students at British, French and other Western European universities and Russian researchers and (mostly young) businesspeople are present in modest numbers too. Reportedly, in 2001 the EU15 countries were issuing about one million visas a year to Russian citizens.[20]

Compared to the movement of people across national borders within the EU, this is not a large number, out of a Russian population of 144 million. No doubt many of the visas issued each year are repeat visas issued to the same people. But if (say) a total of four million Russian citizens had visited countries in the present EU over the past decade, that would be a more-than-negligible part of the population (just under 3%). A fairly substantial chunk of the Russian business and political elite would appear to have some contacts with and experience of Western Europe. Contacts with the US are much less frequent: in fiscal year 2001 the US Immigration and Naturalisation Service recorded 20,413 immigrants from Russia and 126,564 non-immigrant admissions.[21]

---

[20] The Belgian Ambassador to Russia speaking on November 13, 2001, quoted in *RFE/RL Newsline*, November 14, 2001.

[21] See: www.ins.usdoj.gov/graphics/aboutins/statistics/TEMP01yrbk/TEMPExcel/ (retrieved 05.02.2003).

All in all, Europe matters economically to Russia much more than any other part of the world. Europe in this context means the enlarged EU of 25 nations plus countries closely associated with the EU, namely Norway and Switzerland. Norway, as a member of the European Economic Area, has undertaken to adhere to the EU *acquis* except for the part specifically to do with membership. Switzerland is outside the EEA but has seven sectoral agreements with the EU, the breaching of any one of which would render the others null and void; so it, too, is closely associated with and in many respects is inside the single market.

The next section, therefore, is focused on Russia's relations with the EU.

Russia-EU Economic Issues

Issues not related to EU Enlargement

Russia has until recently been in the peripheral vision, at most, of European Commission staff. They have had more pressing concerns: the single market, the euro, enlargement. Besides, oil and gas apart, Russia is of little significance as a trade partner (Table 2). This may be changing, but Brussels' attention for Russia is still wavering; so, it seems, are its intentions. The rapidity of change, lately, in EU official positions on Russia, is striking.

In January 2002 Pascal Lamy, the EU Trade Commissioner, observed that Russia was becoming a priority in future EU economic policy.[22] This somewhat implausible declaration was based, according to Lamy, on three concerns: the implementation of the EU-Russia Partnership and Cooperation Agreement (which dates from 1994); negotiations for Russian accession to the World Trade Organisation; and the declared EU aim, formally stated in 1999, of establishing (at some unspecified date) a unified economic area embracing an enlarged EU and Russia. To this list, one might add the question of EU recognition of Russia as a market economy. This had not taken place at the time of Lamy's statement and such recognition would need to precede Russian accession to the WTO, and the latter in turn would have to precede the establishment of a single economic space linking Russia and the EU.

One key issue between Russia and the EU is the level of Russian domestic energy prices. Many EU officials see these as providing hidden subsidies to Russian producers. In December 2001 Trade Commissioner Lamy said that the EU would recognise Russia as a market economy only if it ceased levying export duties (which are mainly on oil) and ended its two-tier pricing of energy.[23]

These were and still are very difficult conditions for any Russian leadership to meet. To start with, the situation is different in different parts of the fuel-

---

[22] *BBC Global Newsline FSU Economic*, January 13, 2002.
[23] *RFE/RL Newsline*, December 6, 2001.

energy sector. Oil export volumes are constrained by pipeline capacity, so producers cannot freely switch from home to foreign markets across the whole range of oil production and domestic prices are comparatively low, but not controlled. Domestic gas prices are controlled, on the basis that Gazprom is a monopoly, but it is not necessarily the case that domestic prices are below long-run marginal cost. Domestic electricity prices have indeed been controlled (again on monopoly grounds) and, in this case, prices have clearly been below both market-clearing and cost-recovery levels.

The predominant interpretation by specialists – not just by Eurocrats – of Russian domestic energy prices has been that they incorporate a large quasi-subsidy to Russian producers of manufactures and services.[24] Gas and electricity are the instances usually cited. However, there is now some evidence that gas prices are not "artificially" low. Domestic electricity prices were partially deregulated in early 2003, in ways that may turn out to be quite damaging to households and producers in some regions.[25]

There is also a problem with the logic of any demand that Russia's internal energy (or any other) prices should "equal" world prices. Russia, like other developing countries, has a medium-term equilibrium exchange rate that is much less favourable to the rouble than purchasing power parity. To insist on its domestic energy prices being equivalent at the exchange rate to world prices means requiring them to be high relative to other prices, in an international perspective.

Energy prices remain a contentious issue between Russia and the EU but, in the event, they did not block official EU (and US) recognition of Russia as a market economy in 2002. This ought to have brought benefits for Russia, especially from Europe.

In early 2002, before Russia's change of status, the EU had twenty anti-dumping measures in force against Russian products, about half on steel and other metals and about half on chemicals; it also retained the power to impose quotas on Russian textiles and clothing.[26] Politicians and businessmen in Moscow saw this as EU protectionism, helping to lock Russia into its place as a

---

[24] For assessments see: OECD, *Economic Survey of Russia 2002*. Paris, OECD, 2002; Kuboniwa, Masaaki, 'The Hollowing Out of Industry and expansion of Trade Service Sector in Russia: Domestic Factors determining Russia's Presence in the International Markets under Globalisation', paper presented at the AAASS National Convention, Pittsburgh, PA, November 21-24, 2002; Tabata, Shinichiro, 'Flow of Oil and Gas Export Revenues and Their Taxation in Russia', paper presented at the AAASS National Convention, Pittsburgh, PA, November 21-24, 2002.

[25] Rubchenko, Maksim and Dmitriy Sivakov, 'Reforma bez pravitel'stva' in: *Ekspert*, no. 9, March 10, 2003, pp. 16-22.

[26] Hamilton, Carl B., 'Russia's European Economic Integration: Escapism and Realities', Centre for Economic Policy Research Discussion Paper 3840, 2003.

natural-resource supplier. The change of official status to a market economy should have made anti-dumping measures, in particular, more difficult to bring into play.

Early signs, however, were not good. Russia's status as a market economy came into effect, so far as the EU was concerned, on November 8, 2002; meanwhile, the European Union was adopting amendments to its anti-dumping legislation that reduce the benefit of having market-economy status. Previously, calls for anti-dumping measures against products from companies in a market economy would have to be tested against the costs of those producers, whereas similar complaints about products from a non-market economy could be tested against the costs of supposedly similar producers in third countries. Now, the amended anti-dumping legislation allows the European Commission to raise the prices of supposedly dumped goods from market-economy producers more or less unilaterally if the Commission decides that the original prices are "artificially" low or the country of origin has significant barter trade.[27] EU protectionism is deeply ingrained; so is Brussels' suspicion of Moscow.

There are other economic matters on which piecemeal progress can be made between Russia and the EU, such as the levels of EU quotas on Russian steel or the integration of the Russian and European electricity grids, but the key, longer-term issues concern Russian accession to the WTO, and whether or not Russia is to share a unified economic space with the EU in the foreseeable future.

These two strategic issues are problematic – and linked: it is hard to see how the latter could come about without the former having been settled in Russia's favour. Indeed, in a Russian assessment of Russia's relations with the EU, WTO accession is treated as a step towards the common economic space.[28] At the same time, Russia's WTO accession is not reducible to EU-Russia bilateral negotiations. There are more than 60 WTO members in the working group on Russia's accession. These include the US, Japan and India. All have their own priorities. Reportedly, the US is the most insistent, for example, on the Russian aerospace sector being opened up (one of the trickier accession demands for Russia to accommodate).[29] However, the EU is reported to lead on several key demands.

WTO accession is not merely a matter of working through a list of minor technicalities. The time devoted to it both by President Putin and by Russian industrial lobbies is one indicator of its real significance. It has enormous

[27] *Moscow Times*, November 11, 2002, p. 7.

[28] Mau, V. and V. Novikov, 'Otnosheniya Rossii i ES: prostranstvo vybora ili vybor prostranstva?' in: *Voprosy Ekonomiki*, no. 6, 2002, pp. 133-45.

[29] Cooper, Julian, 'Russia and the WTO', presentation at the Royal Institute of International Affairs, March 21, 2002; see also: Hare, Paul G., 'Russia and the World Trade Organisation' draft, July 2002; the published version, together with contributions by negotiators Lamy and Medvedkov, and by Evgeniy Yasin, is published by the Centre for European Reform at www.cer.org.UK/pdf/p394_Russia_WTO.pdf (accessible from mid-December 2002).

potential importance for the character of the Russian economy. The key out-standing issues, so far as the EU is concerned, are tariff levels, the opening of Russian financial services and telecoms to foreign companies, energy prices and agricultural subsidy levels.[30] Behind these lies the general question of whether or not the Russian economy will be opened up to foreign business, rather than kept as the preserve of the existing Russian business elite – with major implications for the level of competition.

Some specific issues and possible deals include the following: some state support for domestic aerospace continuing, but not by means of tariffs; deregulating domestic gas prices over a transition period; ending restrictions on the nationality of chief executive officers and chief financial officers of companies; export taxes on oil and gas to be replaced by well-head taxes on all production; agricultural subsidy levels to be allowed to increase, but by less than Russia has been seeking.

Compromises are likely to be negotiated. But when? In 2002 President Putin was saying that Russia ought to be able to join the WTO in 2003, ahead of both parliamentary and presidential elections. But the sticking points mentioned above continued to stick well into 2003.[31] The WTO members, meanwhile, ran into delays in the Doha round of trade liberalisation negotiations.[32] It may be difficult to wrap up Russian accession until Doha is settled – 2005, at best. And one of the most active WTO groups pushing for Russian concessions in the accession negotiations has been the European Union.

Yet the establishment of a single EU-Russia economic space, if it makes sense at all, is hardly conceivable before Russia is admitted to the WTO. More-over, WTO accession may be a necessary step towards a single EU-Russia economic space, but is hardly going to be sufficient. Indeed, many knowledgeable people treat the idea of this single economic space as something so remote from practical possibilities as not to be worth discussion. EU policymakers may wish to treat it as a focus for EU-Russia cooperation, but it may be an unhelpful distraction from the practical question of a Russia-EU free trade area.

Commission pronouncements tend to treat a Russia-EU common economic space as something akin to the existing European Economic Area (EEA), combining the EU with Iceland and Norway. That entails an emphasis on approximating laws and policies, with no permanent derogation from the EU's *acquis communautaire* and it would probably, for Russia, exclude free trade in farm products.

In Western Europe, views on this approach vary substantially. One view is that such an EU-dominated arrangement would probably be unacceptable

[30] *Vedomosti*, April 14, 2003.
[31] Compare Hare, Paul G., *o.c.*, 2002; with *Vedomosti* April 14, 2003.
[32] *Economist*, March 29, 2003, pp. 75-77.

for Russia and a comprehensive free trade area would be more helpful. Hamilton points out, among other things, that success for any country in selling to the EU is attributable primarily to that country having strong, competitive producers: he cites the example of the Asian newly-industrialised countries. Harmonizing legislation and regulations is not the point – unless the country engaged in such harmonisation is a candidate to join the EU.[33]

Jacques Sapir argues almost the opposite: that genuinely free trade will lock Russia into a raw-materials-and-energy-supply role and that an active industrial policy should first be pursued in Russia; he doubts, however, the European Commission's capacity to contribute effectively to such a policy.[34]

Samson and Greffe, writing as semi-official advisors to both Brussels and Moscow, argue for the harmonisation of legislation and the establishment of a single economic space, rather than the pursuit of a free trade area, but they accept that not all of the *acquis* is appropriate to Russia now and its adoption should be selective – though they imply that eventually complete harmonisation is desirable. They cite econometric results purporting to demonstrate that the creation of a single market would benefit Russia more than a free trade area would.[35] Since the calculations assume productivity-enhancing effects from a single market, this is not a surprising conclusion.

If a Common European Economic Space included a genuinely and completely free trade area between Russia and the EU, much of this discussion would be superfluous. The trouble with Brussels' notion of a common economic space is that it seems to entail much "harmonisation" by Russia towards rules and regulations unilaterally set by Brussels, together with less than free trade in (presumably) those sectors in which EU producers fear cheap competition, such as steel, some non-ferrous metals, textiles, basic chemicals and farm products.

The problem for any neighbouring, non-member state is that the EU is protectionist. Its common external tariff is modest: a 7% simple average of tariff rates. But, as Åslund and Warner have shown, EU protectionism on agricultural products (17.5% tariff average, with variable levies and technical-standards barriers complicating the picture), steel, chemicals and other "sensitive" sectors (anti-dumping measures readily used and acting as a deterrent in investment in capacity to export to the EU) particularly affects the CIS countries.[36]

---

[33] Hamilton, Carl B., *o.c.*

[34] Sapir, Jacques, 'Russia's Economic Growth and European Integration', paper presented at AAASS National Convention, Pittsburgh, PA, November 21-24, 2002.

[35] Samson, Ivan and Xavier Greffe, *o.c.*

[36] Åslund, Anders and Andrew Warner, 'The Enlargement of the European Union. Consequences for the CIS Countries', Carnegie Endowment for International Peace, Working Paper no. 36, April 2003.

Meanwhile, some Russian policy analysts are taking a robust view of the relationship between Brussels and Moscow. Mau and Novikov consider the steps towards first a free trade area and then a single market. They treat institutional compatibility as the key issue. But they advocate a highly selective Russian adoption of the European Union's *acquis communautaire*. They argue that much of what is being required of the EU applicant countries is either not relevant to Russia or would be positively harmful. In particular, they contend that adoption of the *acquis* on labour and social legislation, consumer protection, agriculture and the environment would damage Russia's development as a competitive market economy and is not needed for the creation of a single economic space in which goods, services, labour and capital move freely. Other chapters of the *acquis*, on transport, energy, statistics, telecoms, would be useful but are not necessary. Russia, in their view, can become integrated with Europe, in the sense of the EU, without either joining or even adopting most of the *acquis* like Norway.[37] Their classification of the *acquis* chapters, from the point of view of Russian institutional adaptation, is shown in Table 4.

Table 4. Does Russia need the acquis? The Mau-Novikov view (cells in table are chapters of the acquis, with their numbers)[38]

Irrelevant	Inappropriate	Useful but not essential	Desirable
11. EMU	6. Competition*	9 Transport policy	1. Free movement of goods
15. Industrial policy	7. Agriculture	12. Statistics	2. Free movement of people
16. SMEs	8. Fisheries	14. Energy	3. Free trade in services
17. Science	10. Taxation	19. Telecoms, IT	4. Free movement of capital.
18. Education	13. Social policy	20. Culture, etc	5. Company law
21. Regional policy	22. Environment	26. External relations	6. State aid *
24. Justice, etc	23. Consumer protection		
27. Foreign policy			
28. Financial control			
29. Finance and budget			
30. (EU) institutions.			

Note: * Within Chapter 6, EU competition policy is treated as inappropriate but EU limitations on state aid are accepted as necessary

The Mau-Novikov view of the *acquis* has its supporters outside Russia. Paul Hare, for example, in an analysis of institutional change in transition, notes in passing that the *acquis* has been influential, but perhaps not always in desirable ways.[39] Hamilton's paper, already cited, makes the point that

[37] Mau V. and V. Novikov, *o.c.*
[38] *Source*: Mau V. and V. Novikov, *o.c.*, p. 142.
[39] Hare, Paul G., 'Institutional Change and Economic Performance in the Transition Economies' in: UN ECE, *Economic Survey of Europe*, Issue 2, 2001, pp. 77-94.

harmonisation of the kind espoused by the European Commission entails an unequal jurisdictional relationship – problematic for Norway and no doubt even more problematic for a state that twelve years ago was the core of a superpower.[40]

European Commission officials and most governments in EU member-states will not agree. If there were to be an EU-Russia single economic space in which people move freely, for example, there will be demands that the Russian state also take on EU member-state obligations on social policy and on cooperation in justice and internal affairs. A free trade area that extended to farm products and services would be mutually beneficial but would not raise such difficult issues for Russia.

It may be that Russia has little option but to pursue some sort of "modified EEA" arrangement. Bordachev argues this. Starting with the implicit assumption that closer economic links with Europe are desirable, he considers three possibilities: EU trade preferences such as are provided to North African countries; "perpetual candidate" status, like Turkey; and modified EEA association. The last he treats as the least undesirable and tolerable for Moscow provided inter-parliamentary cooperation can be used to give Russia a say in "pre-draft" discussion of legislation and Russian business groups establish themselves as serious lobbyists in Brussels.[41]

But is a so-called "Common Space" that does not include genuinely free trade in everything really such an attractive deal? Is it possible that the European Union is too *étatiste* for an emerging liberal, dynamic Russian economy to be integrated into it to Russia's advantage? The question may seem far-fetched: where is this dynamic, liberal new Russian economy at present? If analysts and policy advisers like Vladimir Mau - a close associate of Egor Gaidar and formerly head of the government's Working Centre of Economic Reform, now Rector of the Academy of the National Economy - have their way, however, it could yet materialise. That may indeed be rather more likely than a liberalised European Union.

The single economic space, though a long-term and uncertain prospect, should be taken seriously, but it should not be an arrangement dominated by the EU and its problematic *acquis*. Working towards a comprehensive free trade area is more promising. Even that, however, raises additional questions. Could a Russia-EU free trade area work, for example, regardless of conditions in the countries that would border it and which straddle many of the transport routes between Russia and an enlarged EU? Russian territory will adjoin an enlarged EU along borders with Finland, Estonia and (around Kaliningrad) Lithuania and Poland. Elsewhere, Belarus, Ukraine, Moldova and Romania intervene. Can these inconveniently-located transition laggards simply be ignored?

---

[40] Hamilton, Carl B., *o.c.*
[41] Bordachev, Timofey, 'Proshchay, starushka Evropa' in: *Vedomosti*, April 16, 2003.

The US must, compared to the EU, seem a more straightforward partner: its elite thinking is more in harmony with that of Russia both on terrorism and on free markets. It is, however, far less economically engaged with Russia and is likely to remain so. The notion of Russia joining a Free Trade Area for the Americas does not look a starter.[42] If Mercosur countries would not be welcome in such a trade bloc, what price Russia? What is striking is that the Russian establishment's impatience with Europe is strong enough to give such ideas an airing.

The dilemma for Russia is that nobody sees it as a potential EU member in the foreseeable future, but being simply a neighbour to Europe is awkward and (so far) rather unrewarding. Europe is just about prepared to swallow Poland, writes Vladimir Videman, but that is the limit; Ukraine, let alone Russia, would be too much: "it is desirable to absorb into the European order small national enclaves, but certainly not large-scale, multi-cultural blocs."[43] The problem, writes Svetlov, is not even the economic instability of Ukraine and Russia, but the fear that they "will pull the blanket over to their side."[44]

Such speculations about thinking in Western Europe may not be entirely convincing, but they reveal an understandable fear: that Russia will have to fend for itself.[45]

EU Enlargement and Russia

In many respects, the accession of eight Central-East European countries to the EU in 2004 changes very little as far as Russia is concerned.[46]

The main economic effects, potentially, for Russia are the following. The EU market will be larger – but only by about 4% in dollar terms (9% if the combined GDP is measured at purchasing power parity, but for trading purposes it is the exchange-rate measure that counts). Accession may enhance the prosperity of the new members (over and above growth that would have occurred outside the EU), bringing trade-creating effects for third parties. This enhanced prosperity could come from increased productivity in the new members through improved static efficiency, scale effects and possibly competition effects, as well as from dynamic effects through the stimulation of investment. Insofar as the enlargement confers similar benefits (net) on the EU15, there would be similar trade-creating effects there too. Accession may alter the terms of Russian market access to the accession-candidate countries. Finally, the eastward movement of the EU changes the character of the Russian

---

[42] Videman (Widdemann), Vladimir, 'Okno v Evropu ili dver' v Ameriku' in: *Ekspert*, no. 9 March 10, 2003, pp. 59-65.

[43] *Ibid.*

[44] Svetlov, R.V., *Druz'ya i vragi Rossii.* St Petersburg, Amfora, 2002, p. 56.

[45] Khisamov, Iskander, 'Vybor kontserta' in: *Ekspert*, no. 9, March 10, 2003, p. 65.

[46] The accession of Cyprus and Malta can be ignored here, except to note that a large amount of offshore Russian capital would join the EU with the first of these two Mediterranean islands.

border around Kaliningrad (on both sides, if Poland and Lithuania both accede in 2004 or thereabouts): this will affect border trade and therefore the economy of Kaliningrad.

On the whole, these effects cannot be very serious. In any case, they have in part already come to pass. The change in the size of the EU market is minor. Åslund and Warner present enlargement as highly significant for Russia and the other CIS countries, but what they have to say is not in fact at odds with the assessment here. Their argument is that the protectionism of the EU has significant costs for the CIS countries (see the previous section), and that enlargement highlights the difference in treatment between the new insiders (the accession countries) and those that remain outside. Their analysis and evidence do not bear on the cost of enlargement itself. In fact they speculate that enlargement might operate as a stimulus to accelerate reform in the CIS countries – a conjecture that might just as easily be turned on its head: exclusion could breed a defiant rejection of attempts to be more like those included.[47]

The main point here is that many of the effects of enlargement for Central Europe – and indirectly for Russia – have already begun to appear. Most trade between the leading accession candidates and the EU is already free. The Central-East European countries' (CEECs') trade shifted sharply westwards after the collapse of communism. This re-orientation has been assisted by the CEECs' associate status with the EU and the elimination of most trade barriers. Still, it must be largely attributed to the re-assertion of the force of gravity after the removal of central planning: the influences of competitiveness, market size and transport costs were allowed to operate on the CEECs' economies after the collapse of the Soviet-dominated Council for Mutual Economic Assistance.

In some cases, transport systems have been or are being reshaped to facilitate this. For example, the CEECs' electricity grids, formerly integrated with the Soviet grid, are now linked with the Scandinavian (Nordel) or West European (UCPTE) grids – and these two are now being combined; this increases the urgency of Russia's interest in linking its grid with the new Trans-European Synchronised Integrated System.[48]

Similarly, the stimulation of foreign direct investment into the CEECs (including from Russia), to be expected of accession, must to a large extent already be in operation.

Thus, some of the effects associated with accession are already being felt in the accession countries. The static-efficiency effects of freer trade, worth probably only about 1% of GDP,[49] have mostly been captured. The ending of

[47] Åslund, Anders and Andrew Warner, o.c.

[48] Kommersant - Daily, March 20, 2002, p.1.

[49] See: Dyker, David, 'The Dynamic Impact on the Central-Eastern European Economies of Accession to the European Union: Social Capability and Technology Absorption' in: Europe-Asia Studies, November 2001, Vol. 53 Issue 7, pp. 1001-21.

EU contingent protection against imports of so-called "sensitive items" is still to come; so are the mixed blessings of the Common Agricultural Policy – from which the new members will get comparatively little in the way of additional subsidies, but more competition.

The benefits of operating in a larger market (scale effects that can be distinguished from pure resource-allocation improvements on the assumption of constant returns) have also been partially captured already and are not substantial.

Competition effects could be positive or negative. Joining the EU is not automatically good for a nation's economic health. A previously backward country may thrive and rapidly narrow the gap between its own development level and that of the most advanced EU members. Or its businesses may struggle and make little headway against strong competition in the new single market. Ireland and Greece, respectively, exemplify these two outcomes.

Joining a single market and, in due course, the eurozone as well, should stimulate investment by reducing country risk. Dyker cites an estimate of an output boost of up to 19% resulting from this.[50] It does seem likely that the eight leading CEEC accession candidates, whose growth already exceeds that of the EU15, should if anything be more Irish than Greek in this respect. But again, this is a benefit already being perceived. The prospect of accession has already stimulated inward foreign investment into the CEECs – and probably domestic investment as well.

In short, the trade-creating effects, for Russia, of a Central-Eastern Europe rendered more prosperous by joining the EU are not huge and, in any case, are already operating in part. The small economic size of the CEECs suggests that corresponding net gains for the EU15 from the enlargement will also not be very large. By the same token, any such benefits have already been partly captured.

What about trade diversion? Could Russian products suffer from the accession states' adoption of the common external tariff of the EU in place of their own tariffs? Two Russian specialists, Zakhmatov and Fomichev, address market access issues in the case of Poland. They observe first of all a possibly positive consequence for Russian exports to Poland: on joining the EU, Poland will adopt the EU general system of preference (GSP); Zakhmatov and Fomichev calculate that for 60 out of 62 4-digit tariff headings, the GSP tariffs on Russian goods are lower than Poland's present tariffs; on the other hand, they note, the GSP will lower Polish tariffs for third-world exporters even more, so Russia faces lower tariffs but intensified competition.[51]

---

[50] *Ibid.*

[51] Zakhmatov, Nikolay and Viktor Fomichev, 'Integratsiya Pol'shi v ES i interesy Rossii' in: *Sovremennaya Evropa*, Oct/Dec 2001, http://isn.rsuh.ru/iu/journal (retrieved 30.01.2002).

Hamilton reaches the same conclusion with respect to Poland, but finds that accession and the adoption of the EU common external tariff would slightly raise the trade-weighted average tariff on Russian goods entering Hungary and the Czech Republic. It looks as though any net effect of tariff changes will be close to zero.[52]

Zakhmatov and Fomichev also draw attention to the fact that Poland in 1999 took 87% of its oil imports [and therefore presumably 87% of all its oil usage – PH] from Russia and 75% of its gas. These proportions may be subject to downward pressure because of the EU energy-sourcing policy (unquantified "diversity"). However, they judge that, while proportions taken from Russia may be gradually reduced over time, absolute amounts may change little or could even grow.[53]

The two other consequences they note may be mutually offsetting. Russian problems with EU technical standards will be extended to the Polish market. On the other hand, Russian access via Poland to the EU15 market may be eased; this is because Russia's Partnership and Cooperation Agreement with the EU requires EU members states to allow free (administratively unimpeded) access across their territory to markets in other EU countries. Funding from the European Investment Bank may also be drawn on to improve these transport routes.

The Russian leadership understandably, therefore, wants to develop a constructive relationship with Poland. Speaking in Poznan on January 17, 2002, President Putin said: "Both our countries are interested in the construction on this continent of a single space of stability and progress." He went on to speak of Poland's accession to the EU as providing opportunities for greater economic cooperation between Russia and Poland, observing that Poland's present 5% share in Russian merchandise trade could and should be larger.[54]

The Kaliningrad border issue is significant, although perhaps more for diplomatic and even symbolic than for economic reasons. A new EU border on either side of Kaliningrad will differ from the existing Russia-EU border in Karelia in two ways.

Firstly, the neighbouring states were not long ago in the same economic bloc (in the case of Lithuania, in the same country). By contrast, when Finland joined the EU, it had long been kept at arm's length in its dealings with Moscow. The Karelian border has become softer since then, as things have changed on the eastern side. The new Schengen borders around the Russian exclave are barriers to a thriving legal, semi-legal and illegal cross-border trade between Kaliningrad and its neighbours that has grown over the past decade and probably (no reliable measurement yet exists) matters a great deal to Kaliningrad.

[52] Hamilton, Carl B., o.c.

[53] Zakhmatov, Nikolay and Viktor Fomichev, o.c.

[54] See: www.president.ru/events/436.html (retrieved 25.02.2002).

Secondly, these borders are around a piece of Russian territory already physically separated from the rest of Russia and whose past, as Königsberg, contributes to Moscow's sensitivity about it. President Putin has taken it on himself to call for visa-free travel for Kaliningrad residents through Poland or Lithuania to Russia. By saying this himself, he made it harder for Russia to back down. Yet neither Lithuania nor Poland considers such an arrangement as workable[55] – quite apart from the objections of existing EU member-states. Indications of a readiness to compromise have come from the Russian Prime Minister,[56] but a deal could take a long time.

Despite these hints from the Prime Minister about a possible compromise, the tougher line taken by the President still predominated in late summer 2002. The Defence Minister, Sergey Ivanov, speaking on July 30 in Lithuania, repeated the call for visa-free travel.[57] Dmitriy Rogozin, the Chairman of the Duma International Affairs Committee and a hard-liner on Kaliningrad, was appointed as special presidential envoy in international negotiations about the region; he repeated the demand around the same time.[58] Moreover, he contended that visa-free travel to and from Kaliningrad should be a right of all Russian citizens; some Western proposals for special electronic cards to be issued to Kaliningraders, allowing them visa-free overland access to and from the Russian "mainland", would be discriminatory.[59]

The more conciliatory (unofficial) Western suggestions did not go beyond a soft visa regime or special ID cards for residents of Kaliningrad, facilitating cheap and frequent cross-border travel for legal trading.

A compromise was reached at the Russia-EU summit in Brussels on November 11, 2002. This entailed the adoption of "simplified transit documents" (*uproshchennye tranzitnye dokumenty*, or *UTD*, in Russian) for transit across Lithuania between Kaliningrad and "mainland" Russia. This was a fudge. The *UTDs* are visas by another name. EU taxpayers will cover the cost of the system, so the *UTDs* will be free to Kaliningraders and (at the Lithuanian border) to Russian family members travelling to see relatives in Kaliningrad.[60] Details still have to be worked out, but it is not clear how, if at all, these documents will help cross-border traders – who are, after all, not transiting Poland or Lithuania. The Russian media treated the outcome as a victory for Putin. Some European commentators emphasised, on the contrary, that this was a concession by Putin and that in return the EU had soft-pedalled issues of human rights in Chechnya.[61]

---

[55] *RFE/RL Newsline*, June 11, 2002.
[56] *Ibid.*
[57] Itar-Tass from Palanga, July 30, 2002.
[58] Interfax from Moscow, July 30, 2002.
[59] Radio Russia, August 11, 2002.
[60] See: www.strana.ru, www.Izvestiya.ru of November 11, 2002.
[61] Notably *Le Monde*, November 12, 2002.

More serious and constructive decisions could be made about Kaliningrad. One possibility – ambitious but not necessarily impracticable – is suggested by Evgeny Vinokurov: Kaliningrad as a free trade area within the EU (requiring effective administration of certificates of origin, so that Russian production in total does not flow freely into the EU) and cheap and convenient travel between Kaliningrad and the EU, restricted to Kaliningrad residents on the one hand and EU citizens going only to Kaliningrad on the other hand. Some such special status could bring real benefits for the residents of Kaliningrad and also build confidence between Moscow and Brussels.[62]

Conclusions

Russia's economy has been growing quite strongly. The sustainability of that growth is a matter of dispute. A case can be made that economic institutions are improving and that growth is not reducible to a favourable exchange rate and high o rices. In some respects, the Russian economy is now rather open. More than half of Russia's trade, much of its investment (inward and outward) and much of the Russian people's cross-border contacts are with Europe. Trade is otherwise rather dispersed among trade partners. The US is a minor trade-partner for Russia, but rather more important with respect to investment into Russia and more broadly as an influence on the world trading environment, including in oil and gas.

Russia is economically already quite strongly intertwined with the present EU. Those links are likely to strengthen further. The EU's eastward enlargement will not radically alter the scale of Russia-EU trade and investment flows. Some of the economic consequences for Russia of that enlargement, in fact, are already operating ahead of the enlargement itself.

The main economic issues between Russia and Brussels are EU support for Russian WTO accession and the terms demanded for that support in access to Russian markets and further Russian structural reform; the long-term prospects for a unified economic space spanning Russia and an enlarged EU – which almost certainly requires Russian WTO accession as a pre-condition; and the handling of Kaliningrad in the present enlargement. It has been argued here that Brussels' notion of a common economic space is probably too one-sided, especially in its emphasis on EU partners adopting the *acquis* and its lack of a clear commitment to genuinely free trade.

Negotiations for WTO accession have been arduous and prolonged. WTO members want all sorts of commitments from Russia that they could not be bothered to demand when they admitted Moldova, Kirgizstan, Georgia and

---

[62] Vinokurov, Evgeny, 'What Russia and the EU can do for Kaliningrad and what Kaliningrad can do for the European-Russian Dialogue', Brussels, draft CEPS working document, March 2003.

Armenia. Yet there are other ways of looking at what is at stake: just as Russia's entry has significant consequences, so does its continued exclusion.

Russia's interests are probably not best served by the development of a Common European Economic Space as presently envisaged in Brussels. Current thinking in the European Commission is long on Russian "harmonisation" with the EU and short on opening EU markets to "sensitive" products from Russia – which now include grain.

Two scenarios could be envisaged. The first would entail long delays over the WTO, relegating the single economic space or free trade area to some never-never land. The second would be at least a rate of progress on the WTO that kept Russian interest in it alive and which made the achievement of a free trade area within (say) 10-15 years a serious possibility. Just how Kaliningrad is handled is a separable issue. But EU, Polish and Lithuanian generosity over Kaliningrad – stopping short of foolish give-aways creating a border porous to all kinds of *biznes* – would help promote the second scenario.

The first scenario appeals to those West Europeans who are so suspicious of Russia that they fear the consequences of getting close to it, even in its post-communist form. The case for the second scenario rests on a belief that Russia and Europe both gain from closer mutual contact. In choosing between the two, one gets little help from history. An opening up of Russia to Europe and Europe to Russia has never been tried before.

The US is unlikely to play a significant part in Russia's integration into the wider world economy, purely as a trade partner. Its importance to Moscow is above all political – that is, geostrategic. The role of the US Administration and US oil companies in shaping oil and gas development in the Caspian Basin and in the Middle East is also significant for Moscow. But there could be another role for the US in Russia's economic emergence on the world stage: that of a politically powerful interlocutor who goads others, including the EU, into opening up their markets more than they currently do. As a small, open economy outside a major trading bloc, Russia needs powerful friends of this kind. To play this role, the US does, however, need to be serious itself about freer trade.

Bibliography

Åslund, Anders, and Andrew Warner, 'The Enlargement of the European Union. Consequences for the CIS Countries', Carnegie Endowment for International Peace, Working Paper no. 36, April 2003.

Boone, P. and D. Rodionov, 'Rent seeking in Russia and the CIS', paper presented at the tenth anniversary conference of the EBRD, London, December 2001.

Bordachev, Timofey, 'Proshchay, starushka Evropa' in: *Vedomosti*, April 16, 2003.

BP (British Petroleum), *BP statistical review of world energy June 2002*. London, BP, 2002.

Cooper, Julian, 'Russia and the WTO', presentation at the Royal Institute of International Affairs, March 21, 2002.

Dyker, David, 'The Dynamic Impact on the Central-Eastern European Economies of Accession to the European Union: Social Capability and Technology Absorption' in: *Europe-Asia Studies*, Vol. 53 Issue 7, November 2001.

EC Green Paper, *Towards a European strategy for the security of energy supply*. European Commission, 2000, available at http://europe.eu.int/comm/energy_transport/en/lpi_en_3.html

EU-Russia Energy Partnership. European Commission, 2002, *ibid*.

Grabbe, Heather, *Profiting from EU Enlargement*. London, Centre for European Reform, 2001.

Hamilton, Carl B., 'Russia's European Economic Integration: Escapism and Realities', Centre for Economic Policy Research Discussion Paper 3840, 2003.

Hanson, Philip, 'The Russian Economic Recovery: Do Four Years' Growth Tell us that the Fundamentals have Changed?' in: *Europe-Asia Studies*, Vol. 55 Issue 3, May 2003.

Hanson, Philip, and Michael Bradshaw (eds.), *Regional Economic Change in Russia*. Cheltenham, Edward Elgar, 2000.

Hare, Paul G., 'Institutional Change and Economic Performance in the Transition Economies' in: UN ECE, *Economic Survey of Europe* 2002, no. 2, 2001.

Holzman, Franklyn D., 'Foreign Trade' in: A. Bergson and S. Kuznets (eds.), *Economic Trends in the Soviet Union*. Cambridge Mass., Harvard University Press, 1963.

Khisamov, Iskander, 'Vybor kontserta' in: *Ekspert*, no. 9, March 10, 2003.

Kuboniwa, Masaaki, 'The Hollowing Out of Industry and expansion of Trade Service Sector in Russia: Domestic Factors determining Russia's Presence in the International Markets under Globalisation', paper presented at the AAASS National Convention, Pittsburgh, PA, November 21-24, 2002.

Liuhto, Kari, 'Russian Oil and Gas – A Source of Integration', Research Report, Dept. of Industrial Engineering and Management, Lappeenranta University of Technology, 2002.

Mau, V. and V. Novikov, 'Otnosheniya Rossii i ES: prostranstvo vybora ili vybor prostranstva?' in: *Voprosy ekonomiki*, no. 6, 2002.

OECD, *Economic Survey of Russia 2002*. Paris, OECD, 2002.

Rautava, Jouko, 'The Role of Oil Prices and the Real Exchange Rate in Russia's Economy', Bank of Finland, BOFIT Discussion Paper no. 3, 2002.

Rubchenko, Maksim and Dmitriy Sivakov, 'Reforma bez pravitel'stva' in: *Ekspert*, no. 9, March 10, 2003.

Samson, Ivan and Xavier Greffe, *Common Economic Space: Prospects of Russia-EU Relations. White Book*. Moscow, TACIS/RECEP, 2002.

Sapir, Jacques, 'Russia's Economic Growth and European Integration', paper presented at AAASS National Convention, Pittsburgh, PA, November 21-24, 2002.

Sulamaa, Pekka, and Mika Widgren, 'Eastern Enlargement and Beyond: A Simulation Study on EU and CIS integration', Centre for Economic Policy Research Discussion Paper 3768, 2003.

Svetlov, R.V., *Druz'ya i vragi Rossii*. St.-Petersburg, Amfora, 2002.

Tabata, Shinichiro, 'Flow of Oil and Gas Export Revenues and Their Taxation in Russia', paper presented at the AAASS National Convention, Pittsburgh, PA, November 21-24, 2002.

Telehami, Shibley, *et al.* (exchange of views), 'Does Saudi Arabia Still Matter?' in: *Foreign Affairs*, Vol. 81 Issue 6, Nov-Dec. 2002.

Videman (Widdemann), Vladimir, 'Okno v Evropu ili dver' v Ameriku' in: *Ekspert*, no. 9, March 10, 2003.

Vinokurov, Evgeny, 'What Russia and the EU can do for Kaliningrad and what Kaliningrad can do for the European-Russian Dialogue', Brussels, draft CEPS working document, March 2003.

Zakhmatov, Nikolay, and Viktor Fomichev, 'Integratsiya Pol'shi v ES i interesy Rossii' in: *Sovremennaya Evropa*, Oct-Dec. 2001.

THE CONTRIBUTORS

Geoffrey Hosking is Leverhulme Research Professor in Russian History at the School of Slavonic & East European Studies of the University College London. His research concerns the history of Russia and the Soviet Union, nation-building and state-building in Russia, the ex-Soviet Union from 1991, and society, ideology and literature in the Soviet Union. He published a number of articles and books on these subjects, of which his principal publications are *A History of the Soviet Union* (3rd edition,1992), *Russia: People and Empire* (1997), and *Russia and the Russians: a history from Rus to Russian Federation* (Harvard University Press and Allen Lane Penguin Press, 2001).

Wim Coudenys (Brugge, °1966) is a Postdoctoral Fellow of the Fund for Scientific Research - Flanders and is a Lecturer of Russian History at the Katholieke Universiteit Leuven. He specializes in the field of Belgo-Russian relations and has extensively published on the subject. He is the author of *Ivan Nazjivin, Rus, schrijver en emigrant* (1999) and co-author of *Puškin v Flandrii 1799-1999* (1999). His history of the Russian emigration in Belgium, 1917-1945 is due out next year.

Irina M. Busygina is Professor at the School of Political Science at MGIMO, Moscow. She teaches Political Geography, Regional Political Studies and European Integration. Until 1999, she was Head of the Division for Regional an Social Problems at the Institute of Europe in Moscow. Her fields of research are Russian and German federalism, centre/periphery relations (Russian and European perspective), regional identity, and regional policy. Professor Busygina has over 70 publications, the most recent ones being 'Conceptual Basics of European Regionalism' in: *Regions and Regionalism in the West and Russia.* (Moscow, 2001), 'Russian Regional Institutions in the Context of Globalization and Regionalization' in: *Explaining Post-Soviet Patchworks.* (Ed. by Klaus Segbers. Aldershot UK, 2001) (with N. Zubarevich), 'Russia's Regions in Search of Identity' in: *Acta Slavica Iaponica*, (Tomus XIX 2002, Hokkaido, Japan).

John Löwenhardt obtained his Ph.D. in Political and Social Science (Sovietology) at the University of Amsterdam. He was linked at the Institute of Russian and East European Studies of the University of Amsterdam and the Institute of East European Law and Russian Studies of the University of Leiden (The Netherlands) before becoming Alexander Nove Professor of Russian and East European Studies and Director of the Institute of Central and East European Studies at the University of Glasgow (1997-2002). In 1995 he published *The Reincarnation of Russia: Struggling with the Legacy of Communism, 1990-1994.* (Durham N.C., Duke University Press), in 1998 he edited the volume on *Party Politics in Post–Communist Russia* and in 2001 (with David Betz) *Army and State in Postcommunist Europe* (both: London & Portland, Frank Cass). John

Löwenhardt recently joined the Netherlands Institute of International Affairs Clingendael in The Hague where his current research is focused on the foreign and security policies of Russia, Ukraine, Belarus and Moldova, and relations among them.

Irina Kobrinskaya (°1952) studied English Philology at the Moscow State University. Since 1975 she is joint as a research fellow at the Institute of US and Canada Studies of the Russian Academy of Science where she obtained her Ph.D. in International Relations. She worked as a Senior research Fellow at the Institute of Political studies of the Polish Academy of Science in Warsaw (1989-1992), as a researcher and program coordinator at the Moscow Carnegie Endowment (1994-1997), and as an analyst and commentator for radio and Russian National TV. In 1998, she founded the Moscow Centre of the New York East-West Institute, which she directed until January 2001. At present she is Executive Director of the Foundation for Prospective Studies and Initiatives in Moscow and heads the section on European Security at the Institute of Europe of the Russian Academy of Sciences.

Irina Kobrinskaya conducts her research in the following fields: Russian domestic and foreign policy, domestic factors of foreign security decision-making, military reform and civil-military relations, international security, peace-making, think thanks in policy decision-making, mass media in policy decision and public opinion making, Russia-NIS and Central Eastern European states relations, and Russia-USA, Russia-EU and Russia-NATO relations.

She is the author of four and co-author of nearly 30 monographs on these topics and has written more than 100 articles in periodicals on domestic policy, foreign policy, and international security that have been published in Russia, the United States an Europe.

Philip Hanson (°1936) is Professor Emeritus of the Political Economy of Russia & Eastern Europe at the University of Birmingham. He worked as Senior Economic Affairs Officer for the United Nations Economic Commission for Europe in Geneva (1991-92) and as visiting Professor of Economics at the University of Michigan and at the Kyoto Institute of Economic Research. In 2001-02 he was Director of the Centre for Russian and East European Studies in Birmingham.

His recent work has been on regional patterns of economic change in post-communist Russia, on the economic history of the Soviet Union 1945-1991, on Russia-EU economic relations and on contemporary Russian economic policy. He published a number of journal articles on these topics in *Europe-Asia Studies, European Economic Review, Post-Communist Economies, Problemy prognozirovaniya, Economy and Society* and elsewhere. His books include *Trade and Technology in Soviet-Western Relations* (London: Macmillan & New York: Columbia University Press, 1981), *The Comparative Economics of Research Development and Innovation in East and West: A Survey* (with Keith Pavitt, Chur: Harwood Academic Publishers, 1987), *Western Economic Statecraft in East-West Relations: Embargoes, Sanctions, Linkage, Economic Warfare, and Détente* (London:

Routledge and Kegan Paul, 1988), *From Stagnation to Catastroika* (Washington, DC: CSIS, 1992) and *Regional Economic Change in Russia* (co-edited with Michael Bradshaw, Cheltenham: Edward Elgar, 2000). His articles regularly appear in *Financial Times, Independent* and *Times.*

THE EDITORS

Katlijn Malfliet (°1954) studied Law and philosophy at the Catholic University of Leuven. After obtaining a MA in Eastern European Studies (RUG-KUL-VUB), she wrote her doctoral thesis on property Law in the Soviet Union among others at the Academy of Sciences in Moscow. She studied Russian in Leuven, Brussels and Moscow. As visiting professor she taught at the universities of Leiden, Moscow and Prague. At the Catholic University of Leuven, she teaches courses on political, social and juridical transition in Central and Eastern Europe.

As research director for Central and Eastern Europe of the Institute for International and European Policy, professor Malfliet leads several research and development projects about transition in the post-communist countries (mainly the Russian Federation). The main research topics are: privatisation and institutional reform and the link between culture, politics and law. Professor Malfliet wrote several books on these topics: *De moeilijke weg naar democratie en markt in Midden-en Oost-Europa* (Davidsfonds, 1993) ; *Intellectual Property Rights in Russia : A System in Transition* (Bruylant, 1994) ; *Alternatieven voor het teloorgegane communisme* (ed.), (Garant, 1994) ; *Regionalism in Russia* (IEB, 1995) ; *Towards the Rule of Law in Russia* (IEB, 1996) ; *Wie is bang voor Oost-Europa ?* (ed.), (Garant, 1997) ; *Minority Policy in Central and Eastern Europe* (co-edited with R. Laenen, Garant, 1998) ; *Is Russia a European Power ? The Position of Russia in a New Europe.* (co-edited with T. Casier, Leuven University Press, 1999) ; *Het Europees Beleid van Rusland* (co-edited with L. Verpoest, Garant, 2000), and *Russia and Europe in a Changing International Environment* (co-edited with L. Verpoest, Leuven University Press, 2001).

Francisca Scharpé (°1978) studied Eastern European Languages and Cultures at the University of Ghent and the Humboldt University of Berlin (1996-2000). After obtaining her Masters degree, she was rewarded a scholarship by the Flemish Community for a post-graduate study of Russian Language at the Saint-Petersburg State University. Additionally she studied law at the Université Robert Schuman in Strasbourg and the Free University of Brussels. She now coordinates the activities of the Chair Interbrew – Baillet Latour on the relations between Russia and the European Union and conducts in this framework research on Human Rights in Russia and the influence of Russia's membership to the Council of Europe and to the CIS on Human Rights protection in Russia.

www.ingramcontent.com/pod-product-compliance
Lightning Source LLC
Chambersburg PA
CBHW070255290326
41930CB00041B/2541